50 DRAMA SKETCHES FOR YOUTH

50 Drama Sketches for Youth

NICK PAGE

GREAT IDEAS

EASTBOURNE

First published 2003

ISBN 1 84291 045 0

Published by
KINGSWAY COMMUNICATIONS LTD
Lottbridge Drove, Eastbourne BN23 6NT, England.
Email: books@kingsway.co.uk

Book design and production for the publishers by
Bookprint Creative Services, P.O. Box 827, BN21 3YJ, England.
Printed in Great Britain.

Contents

CONTENTS

CONTENTS

Performance and Copyright

The right to perform any of the sketches within this book is included within the cover price, so long as those performances are in an amateur context, for example in church or school. Where any charge is made to the audience, permission in writing must be obtained from the author, who can be contacted through the publishers. A fee may be payable for the right to perform sketches in such circumstances.

The book is copyright, and no part may be copied without permission in writing from the publisher. Where multiple copies of a sketch are required for those playing the parts, it is generally simpler and cheaper to buy extra copies of the book.

Introduction

Tell me a story

'Literature is a luxury; fiction is a necessity' (G. K. Chesterton). Humans love stories. We are addicted to characters and events, to tales of 'what happened next' and 'once upon a time . . .' We love to tell each other stories of what we did at the weekend, what happened to friends of ours, things we read about in the papers or heard on the news, jokes, tall tales. Stories help us to grasp complex issues and imagine what we might do in certain circumstances. They help us to understand other people, and, crucially, to understand more about God: 'Again he said, "What shall we say the kingdom of God is like, or what parable shall we use to describe it?"' (Mark 4:30).

When it comes to telling stories, few methods do this better than drama. Using drama in your youth group can make the issue seem alive and relevant. It can offer the young people you are dealing with the chance to participate, to imagine themselves into certain situations. It can make the Bible come alive.

Here are four compelling reasons you should be using drama in your church or youth group.

It provides examples

A drama is a slice of life, a short story which offers a way into any subject. Or it can be a parable, a metaphor for what God is like or what life is all about. It opens up the discussion in a way few other communication methods can match.

It changes the perspective

Especially when it comes to the Bible, there is a tendency to think, 'Oh, this happened a long time ago.' Drama can place Bible teaching in a different culture, allowing the audience to see the Bible through today's eyes.

It is all about people

Just as drama can update the setting, it can also explore character in a new way. What were the people really like? Drama allows us to understand more about how a bully or their victim might feel, for example, than an abstract discussion.

It speaks their language

Drama is a language that people – especially young people – understand. After all, they all watch soaps, or TV drama, or films. It is a method of communication which, in many cases, is far more accessible to them than a book or a talk from a speaker.

So drama is an incredibly powerful weapon in the war of communication. It tells stories and presents dilemmas in an interesting and exciting way. But when we think about drama, we often shy away from it, expecting it to take a lot of organisation or pre-planning. The good news is that drama is easy to include in any youth group programme. It need not take a lot of rehearsal – you just have to use a little imagination! Here are some tips on how to make it a little easier.

Sketches the easy way

One of the things which puts us off using drama is the preparation time involved. We have to find actors, organise rehearsals, make sure people have learned their lines – and there is enough work involved in church without having to become a theatre producer as well! Which is exactly why I produced these sketches. There is no doubt that, like all scripts, these would work best if learnt and rehearsed and, in an ideal world, performed by people who can actually *act*. However, if you don't have the time or the energy to organise this, there are some simpler ways to use them.

You don't have to learn it

First select some youth group members or leaders who can act a little bit. Give them a copy of the script and a few moments for a read through, and then just have them act it out impromptu, reading from the script. As many of the sketches featured in this book are simple dialogues, this can work surprisingly well.

Of course you can spice this up a bit by issuing the sketch as a challenge to selected, unsuspecting participants. Tell them they can read the sketch from the script but they've got to create the scene from whatever is around them. They can organise some furniture and even borrow bits of clothing or props off other members of the youth group. You'd be surprised how well people rise to the challenge!

Treat it like a radio play

For a sketch with more characters in, present it as a radio play. For instance, have the actors come forward and read their lines into a microphone on cue. You could even appoint someone to be in charge of sound effects.

Read it to each other

Break the group into smaller groups – the same number as the number of characters in the sketch – and have them read through the sketch together. (This is also a good way of dealing with Bible passages, using resources such as *The Dramatised Bible*.)

We're not dealing with Shakespeare here, people. These are simple sketches with the minimum of staging. Enjoy yourselves. Use your imagination. Have *fun*!

Taking it further

One of the best uses of drama is to pose questions and set up dilemmas. These sketches were originally published in *Youthwork* magazine, and each sketch was accompanied by four or five questions to encourage discussion in youth groups. Obviously the most straightforward way of handling this discussion is to have someone perform the sketch and then simply pose the questions to the group. However, there are more inventive ways of using drama in discussion.

Hot seating

The central character or characters from the sketch sits on a seat in front of the group. They are then asked questions by the group and respond in character. Obviously this takes a bit of acting ability, but given a little imagination it is not hard for the actors to enter into the spirit of things.

The action replay

Re-run the sketch, but stop it at certain points. Ask the audience to analyse what is happening by answering questions: Why did he say that? What thoughts are going through his head? How would you react if someone said that to you? What would you do at this point? Then start 'running the tape' again, picking up the sketch where you left off and carrying on to the next point you wish to discuss.

Write a letter

Have the youth group members write a letter to one of the characters in the sketch. Ask them to include some simple pieces of advice about the dilemma that is being presented. Maybe they can suggest things from their own experience that would help the characters.

What if?

It is sometimes interesting to wonder, 'What if . . .' What if the characters had spoken a different way or made a different choice? What would they think about other related issues? Or you can ask the classic 'What happened next?' and get the audience to take the story further.

Author's note

Many of the characters in these sketches are not gender specific. Doctors, shop assistants, customers, firefighters and shepherds can all be played by either male or female actors. So feel free to change things round to suit your cast. Words like 'she', 'he' and 'madam' can all be changed accordingly – you can even change the names if you like.

Also, although I've made suggestions about setting, costumes and props, these are merely a kind of template. Add what you want, take away what you want, adapt the sketch to fit in with what scenery and staging you have available. At the end of the day, all I'm providing is the words. It's up to you what you do with them!

At the end of each sketch, unless otherwise specified,

characters should briefly 'freeze' to indicate that the piece is finished.

Finally, observant readers will soon notice that an alarming number of these sketches are set in a pub. I would like to take this opportunity to point out that I rarely frequent such places. And when I do, it is all in the cause of research. If, however, this causes you any problems, you can easily relocate the offending sketch to a coffee bar or a 'greasy spoon' café.

Mind you, the research won't be half as much fun.

A few thanks

In the writing of any book there are always many people to thank. In particular I'd like to thank John Buckeridge and Steve Adams at *Youthwork* magazine where these sketches first appeared. I am grateful to them for allowing me to reuse them here. I'd also like to thank Richard Herkes at Kingsway for suggesting this book and then for having the enormous patience to wait for me to deliver the manuscript.

Finally, I'd like to thank all those writers and dramatists who have inspired me over the years. I have learnt from you, admired you, reacted to you and been challenged by you.

Mostly, however, I have stolen your jokes.

Sorry about that.

Issues and Dilemmas

The bulk of the sketches in this book were written to provoke discussion. Along the way they may also provoke laughter, irritation and even mild nausea, but mainly they are intended to get a good argument going. Not an argument for the sake of it, of course, but a debate about things that really matter – a discussion about real life.

It has always seemed to me that people – young people especially – want to know what Christianity has to say about real life. They don't want any airy-fairy, pie-in-the-sky (insert your own multi-hyphenated derogatory adjective here) theories. They want to know how they should live. As Christians, therefore, it's vital that we address the issues that really concern them: issues like self-image, love, anger, greed, honesty, money – all the things that we encounter day by day. And the great thing is that Christianity does have something to say about these issues. We trust and believe in a God who took human form, came to earth and got his hands dirty – a God who worked for a living; who sweated in the heat and shivered in the cold; who slept, ate, laughed, cried, chatted, joked, drank, went to parties, spent time with his mates . . .

17

all the things that have made up human life since the very beginning. He is passionately concerned with human beings – and all aspects of their life.

These sketches, therefore, attempt to raise some real issues. They don't offer simplistic solutions; they don't seek to make deep theological points; they are just trying to get people to think about the life they lead, and, more importantly, what God has to say about it.

1. Love Among the Hairdressers

Topic: Love and romance.

Characters: KRYSTAL; SHARON.

Setting: KRYSTAL and SHARON have retreated into the ladies toilets at a club. They spend most of the sketch peering into the mirror, reapplying their make-up. It is best, therefore, to imagine that the mirror is between the cast and the audience.

Props/costume: Krystal's handbag and mobile phone. Both girls are dressed for a night out – the more tasteless the better.

> (KRYSTAL *and* SHARON *are looking into the mirror, re-applying their make-up.*)

KRYSTAL: I wish we'd never come.

SHARON: What do you mean?

KRYSTAL: Well, this place. It's crawling with vermin.

SHARON: (*Looking around her*) Looks all right to me. They've even unblocked the toilets.

KRYSTAL: I wasn't talking about the toilets. I was talking about the dance floor.

SHARON: I thought some of the blokes were quite dishy.

KRYSTAL: You would.

SHARON: What's that supposed to mean?

KRYSTAL: Well, let's face it Sharon, you've never exactly been picky, have you?

SHARON: I resent that incineration. I'm just sowing my wild oats.

KRYSTAL: You've sown enough for a prairie.

SHARON: Well, it's what it's all about, isn't it? Finding a man.

KRYSTAL: Is that all there is? Can't there be more to relationships than a quick dance, four pints of babycham and a game of tonsil hockey every Saturday night?

SHARON: What's come over you? You used to like all that. *(Pause)* It's Kevin, isn't it?

KRYSTAL: *(Emphatically)* No. Well, maybe . . .

SHARON: Oh, Krystal. You should have got over him by now. It's been two whole days.

KRYSTAL: I can't help it, Sharon. He was everything to me. He was a wild, romantic soul, a beautiful free spirit, a prince among men.

SHARON: *(Pause)* He's a welder.

KRYSTAL: I thought we would be together for eternity. A love that never dies.

SHARON: You live in a dream world, you do. You've read too many of those *True Love* magazines.

KRYSTAL: Romance is all that matters in a relationship.

SHARON: Rubbish. Romance is just a bloke's way of getting what he wants.

KRYSTAL: Oh, that's right! Ruin it. Just because you go to the other extreme. Grabbing hold of every bloke who crosses your path. When I see you in action the words 'complete' and 'slapper' spring to mind.

SHARON: I look at it this way. All that matters is the here and now.

KRYSTAL: But isn't there more to relationships than just –

SHARON: What?

KRYSTAL: You know. *(Spelling it out in a whisper)* S . . . E . . . K . . . S.

SHARON: Nah. Of course not.

KRYSTAL: But what about friendship? What about love? What about commitment?

SHARON: It's all a con. All that matters is physical attraction.

KRYSTAL: You make it sound so . . . so . . . basic.

SHARON: You know your trouble, Krystal – you really think life is going to be like in books.

KRYSTAL: Well, what's wrong with that? Why can't it be that way? Why can't we have romance and true love?

SHARON: Oh, grow up. It will never happen, Krystal. It's a figbox of your imagination.

KRYSTAL: I can't help it. I miss Kevin.

(There is a phone ringing. It is KRYSTAL's mobile. She fishes it out of her handbag and answers it.)

KRYSTAL: *(Posh voice)* Krystal Protheroe Hairdressing International. How may I help you? *(Realising)* Kevin? You do? You will? Ohhhhhhh, Kevin! Yes, all right, snookums. Yes. *(Baby voice)* Baby bear lubs you as well. *(She rings off.)* He still loves me, Sharon. He says it's been the longest two days of his life.

SHARON: You're never going to fall for that!

KRYSTAL: I'm going back to him, Sharon. He needs me.

(KRYSTAL exits.)

SHARON: Love! It makes fools of us all.

(SHARON exits.)

TAKING IT FURTHER

Bible Background: 1 Corinthians 13:8–13

1. 'Romance is just a bloke's way of getting what he wants.' What do you think?
2. Where do you think Krystal has got her ideas of love from? Do you think she's being realistic?
3. Is sex all that matters in a relationship?
4. What should we look for in a relationship? How should our beliefs affect our relationships?
5. Is there a love that never ends?

2. The Life and Soul of the Party

Topic: Bullying.

Characters: DENISE; TRACEY; LAUREN.

Setting: The cast sit on the sofa in a living-room. They begin the sketch lively and animated; it is as if they are being interviewed about Jenny. They volunteer more and more information until the truth gradually emerges.

Props/costume: A sofa.

> (*Three girls,* DENISE, TRACEY *and* LAUREN *are sitting on a sofa, telling stories. They are animated and lively.*)

DENISE: Jenny was, like, the life and soul of the party.

TRACEY: She was great. We all liked her.

LAUREN: You know what I liked about Jenny – she could always take a joke.

DENISE: I remember the time she coloured her hair orange.

TRACEY: Or should I say, she *had* her hair coloured orange.

DENISE: It was really funny – she'd been mucking about or something and Tracey had some hair dye.

TRACEY: Yeah, I'd got it from the chemist or somewhere.

LAUREN: And we all got together in the bogs and dyed her hair for her.

DENISE: She was wild about it. Really wild.

LAUREN: What a laugh!

TRACEY: Then there was the time at the fair.

DENISE: *(Excitedly)* Oh, yeah, I remember, when she went on that ride four times running.

LAUREN: And she keeps going 'But I'm scared of heights!' and laughing and screaming.

TRACEY: Well, screaming, mainly.

DENISE: But we wouldn't let her off.

LAUREN: We all had a real laugh about that afterwards.

TRACEY: While she threw up in the bushes.

DENISE: Say what you like about Jenny, she was always one of the girls.

LAUREN: Oh yeah, she didn't hold back.

TRACEY: She loved life, did Jenny. Life and soul of the party.

DENISE: Not that she was perfect. I mean, sometimes she could be a bit, you know, well, not quite with it.

TRACEY: Yeah, I know what you mean. A bit 'soft'.

LAUREN: Some of the things she'd come out with.

DENISE: I mean, any other group of girls wouldn't have had anything to do with her.

TRACEY: But we kept going.

LAUREN: And if sometimes we had to point out where she was going wrong . . .

DENISE: Well, I'm sure she thanked us for it.

TRACEY: But the main thing is we had a laugh, right?

LAUREN: Like that time when Denise trod on her glasses.

DENISE: *(Not really keen on this topic)* Oh yeah.

TRACEY: Well, stamped on her glasses, really.

DENISE: *(Anxiously)* No, I didn't!

LAUREN: Yeah, you did, you took her glasses off and stamped on them.

DENISE: I didn't. Not stamped.

TRACEY: You threw them to the ground and . . .

DENISE: *(Shouting)* No! I mean, I didn't . . . *(Recovering her poise)* And anyway, what about the time Tracey emptied that nail varnish into her bag? What a mess.

TRACEY: *(Defensively)* Well, it was more an accident than anything else.

LAUREN: Accident? You wrecked everything!

TRACEY: *(Accusing)* Well, what about you – you told her that Tony fancied her.

DENISE: And she believed you.

TRACEY: And she went up to him and said something!

DENISE: She was so embarrassed. Went all red and had to run out of the room.

LAUREN: *(Defensively)* Well, she shouldn't have said anything, should she? I didn't know she was going to say anything. She could be so uncool sometimes.

TRACEY: Yeah. *(Pause)* I don't think she had any other friends.

LAUREN: Not real friends.

DENISE: Not like us.

(There is a pause. They all think for a moment.)

LAUREN: She didn't look the type to take it all personally.

DENISE: I mean, we thought she could take a joke.

LAUREN: Instead she took those tablets.

TRACEY: Hundreds of them.

DENISE: And she left this note. Saying it was bullying.

TRACEY: It was never bullying.

LAUREN: I reckon she had some kind of breakdown.

(The others agree with her.)

TRACEY: I mean it was just, you know, practical jokes.

LAUREN: I'm sure it was nothing to do with us.

DENISE: After all, we were her friends.

TRACEY: And she was the life and soul of the party.

TAKING IT FURTHER

Bible Background: Psalm 22:1–31

1. Why do people bully others?
2. 'I thought she could take a joke.' When does joking stop and bullying begin?
3. Why do you think Jenny hung around with these girls?
4. How could Jenny have stopped the bullying?
5. What can you do about bullying in your school or work-place?

3. Sharon, Tony and Dorothy Perkins

Topic: Betrayal. Forgiveness. Love.

Characters: SHARON; JAN.

Setting: A coffee shop. SHARON sits at a table, nursing a coffee.

Props/costume: Table. Two chairs. Two mugs of coffee.

(SHARON is sitting with a coffee. Enter JAN.)

JAN: Shaz, I'm so sorry . . . I just heard.

SHARON: It's OK.

JAN: How could Tony do this? To you of all people?

SHARON: It's just one of those things.

JAN: No. It's worse than that. He's a monster. And she's nothing more than a common . . .

SHARON: *(Interrupting)* Look, I'm OK. Honestly.

JAN: Have you spoken to him?

SHARON: He won't return my calls. I've left messages, but he never gets back to me. I even went round to see him. I think he was in, but he never answered the door.

JAN: I can't believe it. The two-timing, slimy little toad.

SHARON: I'm not angry at him.

JAN: You aren't?

SHARON: No. Of course, I wouldn't be totally devastated if he happened to be mashed to death by a passing bull elephant. But apart from that . . .

27

JAN: How did you find out?

SHARON: I saw them together. They were coming out of Dorothy Perkins. They were holding hands.

JAN: That's awful.

SHARON: Yes.

JAN: Dorothy Perkins, of all places! That woman has no taste.

SHARON: Never mind the shop! They were holding hands! And then they turned and kissed each other. It was like someone had stabbed me. I went cold. Cold all over.

JAN: I'm not surprised.

SHARON: Then Tony looked up and saw me. And the strange thing was I think he really hated me in that moment. Hated me because I'd found him out. Hated me because I'd made him realise what he was doing.

JAN: Oh Shaz, I'm so sorry.

SHARON: I know. *(Starting to cry)* And he never went shopping with me.

JAN: Now, now, none of that. No time for self-pity. We've got to have a plan of action.

SHARON: Action?

JAN: Revenge, Shaz, revenge. What matters now is making him pay.

SHARON: I'm not sure I want to.

JAN: No, Shaz, you've got to be strong. If you're going to get over this kind of betrayal, you have to be tough. It's dog eat dog out there. You have to learn how to get your own back. Eye for an eye and tooth for a tooth, that's what it's all about.

SHARON: But what would happen if we all did that? We'd all end up blind and only able to eat rice pudding.

JAN: How will you ever get over it if you're not as tough as they are?

SHARON: I don't think I will ever get over it. I mean, I bought the dress and everything. It was going to be such a lovely wedding.

JAN: I know. *(Pause)* Still, look on the bright side – at least I won't have to wear that bridesmaid's outfit.

SHARON: What do you mean? You looked lovely.

JAN: Shaz, it was a skin-tight dress in a particularly lurid shade of bright pink. I looked like a pregnant flamingo. I realise that this is possibly not the best time to tell you this, but I hated it.

SHARON: Well, at least one of us is happy.

JAN: Oh come on, I'm just kidding.

SHARON: I love him, Jan. I love him and I always will. How do you forgive something like that? How do you forgive that kind of betrayal?

JAN: You don't, Shaz, that's just my point. You don't forgive and you don't forget. You bide your time, waiting for the moment when they are off-guard. *(Pause)* And then you push them both under a bus. Harsh, but fair.

SHARON: I don't know. At the moment it's like I'm carrying around this great weight. I don't want to carry it all my life, Jan. I want to feel free again. But that kiss. I will never forget that kiss.

TAKING IT FURTHER

Bible Background: Matthew 26:45–54

1. Have you ever felt betrayed by anyone? How do you think Sharon is feeling?
2. 'What matters now is making him pay.' Why does Jan think this?

3. 'How do you forgive that kind of betrayal?' Do you think Sharon should forgive him? If you do, why?
4. Read the Bible Background. How did Jesus react to his betrayal?

4. It's Not My Fault!

Topic: Blame and responsibility.

Characters: TONY; DAVE; TAXI DRIVER.

Setting: A hospital accident and emergency department. TONY and DAVE each sit on a plastic chair, waiting for the taxi to pick them up. They are both bandaged – it is clear they have been in an accident.

Props/costume: Bandages. Chairs.

(TONY and DAVE are sitting in the hospital accident and emergency department waiting-room. They are both bandaged.)

TONY: Look, for the last time it's not my fault!

DAVE: Oh, no, no, of course not. I mean, the way that tree just leapt out at you.

TONY: Do be quiet.

DAVE: You just can't trust them, can you? You're driving along minding your own business when all of a sudden – wham! A pine tree just jumps out right in front of the car.

TONY: Will you shut up! It wasn't my fault.

DAVE: No? Well, whose was it, then?

TONY: There must have been something wrong with the car. Mechanical failure. Some sort of defect.

31

DAVE: The only defect in that car was holding the steering-wheel. You were just going too fast.

TONY: I was not. I've always taken that bend at 90. It's a fast curve. It's not my fault that someone put a new tree there.

DAVE: Well, this is getting us nowhere. The big question is, what are we going to do?

TONY: Do?

DAVE: We have to tell Dad.

TONY: It's perfectly simple. We just have to go in, explain the situation calmly and maturely. Talk to him like the responsible adults we are.

DAVE: (*Pause*) We're going to die, aren't we?

TONY: Maybe we could emigrate.

DAVE: What?

TONY: You know, run away to Australia or somewhere. Start a new life. Get false identities. I hear Timbuktu is very nice this time of year.

DAVE: It's no good – he'd track us down. You know what he's like about that car.

TONY: Well, we'll just have to explain to him. Tell him all this was just your fault.

DAVE: My fault?

TONY: Well, you took the car keys.

DAVE: I didn't take them. They sort of fell into my pocket. It was virtually an accident.

TONY: Well, the problem is, dear brother, we have just experienced *actually* an accident.

DAVE: Well, I can't help it. Maybe I'm a kleptomaniac. I can't help taking things. It's probably hereditary. I'm just a product of original sin. I blame Adam and Eve.

TONY: Oh, right. That'll work well. Sorry, Dad, we

wrecked your car, but it was all Adam and Eve's fault.

DAVE: Maybe he won't notice.

TONY: Dave – there is a twenty-foot pine tree sticking out of the bonnet. I mean, call me Mr Pessimist, but I can't help feeling that most people would notice a little detail like that.

DAVE: Well, perhaps we should just tell the truth.

TONY: Do you mean the 'truthful' kind of truth? Or the 'truth that is mainly the truth but with quite a lot of details still a bit blurry' kind of truth?

DAVE: The whole truth. You know, own up to what we've done. Ask him to forgive us.

TONY: I'm not going to own up to something that isn't my fault.

DAVE: Tony, we took his car without asking. We drove it into a tree. We are responsible.

TONY: I'm not. I never have been. I mean, only this morning he was telling me how irresponsible I was.

DAVE: Honesty is the best policy.

TONY: No, staying alive is the best policy.

DAVE: Look, we just have to face up to our actions. We can't run away from this one.

TONY: *(Accepting it)* No. You're right. We have to face it.

(Enter TAXI DRIVER.*)*

DRIVER: You two waiting for a taxi?

DAVE: Er, yeah. That's us. *(To* TONY*)* So, we're going to go home, tell the truth and face up to the consequences.

TONY: Right.
DRIVER: Where do you want to go to, then?
TONY & DAVE
  TOGETHER: Timbuktu.

TAKING IT FURTHER

Bible Background: Genesis 3

1. Whose fault was this?
2. What should they tell their father?
3. What do you think Dad's reaction will be? Will he forgive them?
4. 'Honesty is the best policy.' Is this true?
5. Read the Bible Background. What does this tell us about facing up to the consequences of our actions? Is it really all Adam and Eve's fault?

5. Good Clean Fun

Topic: Lust.

Characters: SHERRIL; SONIA.

Setting: SHERRIL and SONIA are waiting at a bus stop. It is not necessary to have an actual stop on stage, although you can construct one out of some plastic tubing with a cardboard sign on top. The easiest way, though, is simply to have the two girls at the front of the stage and, every so often, have them checking whether the bus is on its way. Trust me, it's very easy to fool audiences.

Props/costume: SONIA is dressed for a night out with the girls. SHERRIL is dressed more conservatively.

(SHERRIL and SONIA are waiting at the bus stop.)

SONIA: So are you going tonight?
SHERRIL: Going where?
SONIA: To the Apollo. You know. The show.
SHERRIL: What show is that, then?
SONIA: Oh Sherril, I've told you. Honestly, you have the attention span of a goldfish, you really do.
SHERRIL: That is not true. *(She goes to say something, but forgets what she was going to say)* What were we talking about again?
SONIA: I give up with you. The show. You know. The men.
SHERRIL: *(Unenthusiastically)* Oh. That.

35

SONIA: It's going to be great. The Chippendales in their all-new Jane Austen spectacular. Ooh, just the thought of those great hunky bodies, all oiled and glistening, dressed up in frock coats and riding boots.

SHERRIL: Yes, well, I'm not sure about it.

SONIA: Not sure about it? What's the problem?

SHERRIL: Well, I don't know if I want to watch a load of steroid-pumped blokes taking their shirts off. I'd rather stay in with Kevin.

SONIA: Let me get this straight. You'd rather spend an evening with Kevin? A boy who makes Woody Allen look like Arnold Schwarzenegger?

SHERRIL: He's not that bad.

SONIA: Sherril, he gets exhausted picking up the Sunday papers. He opens a milk carton and he has to go and have a lie-down.

SHERRIL: Well, surprise you as it may, Sonia, I don't go out with Kevin for his muscles.

SONIA: Just as well. I've seen stick insects with better physiques.

SHERRIL: Oh, and Bernie's a Greek god, I suppose.

SONIA: Of course not. *(Thinks)* Well, not unless there's a Greek god of slobs. But that's the point, Sherril. That's why women go and watch these shows. Take your mind off reality. Escape for a while from the Kevins and the Bernies.

SHERRIL: But I don't want to escape.

SONIA: Oh, don't be daft. Everyone wants to escape. Everybody likes to have a bit of a daydream.

SHERRIL: Well, maybe. But maybe there are some places we shouldn't escape to. I mean, maybe there are daydreams that are bad for us, that just unsettle us . . . Oh, I don't know. I just don't like the thought of it, that's all.

SONIA: I really don't know what's come over you. I mean, it's only a bit of fun. It's not like it's pornographic or anything.

SHERRIL: What do you mean? A load of blokes who have been bathing in baby oil take their clothes off and it's not pornographic?

SONIA: No! It's just a giggle, innit? It's like Page Three for the blokes. It's not really wrong. It's just innocent fun.

SHERRIL: Well, I'm not sure. I mean, how would you like it if Bernie went to see a stripper?

SONIA: Sherril – this is not the same. It's been clinically proven that women don't think about these things in the same way. Men go to strippers to lust after them. We don't lust. We . . . we . . .

SHERRIL: Yes?

SONIA: We have a laugh, don't we? Just a giggle. Just good clean fun.

SHERRIL: So if one of these guys picked you out and asked you for a date, you wouldn't go with him?

SONIA: Wouldn't I? You wouldn't see me for dust. *(Realising)* No, no, of course I wouldn't. I am committed to Bernie. Worse luck.

SHERRIL: *(Making up her mind)* I'm not going. There is more to a relationship than physical appearances, Sonia. I like him. We have a laugh. That's the problem with these shows. They reduce everything to appearance. Human beings become lumps of meat. It's degrading. It's like a cattle market.

SONIA: Yes, well, it doesn't hurt anyone to have a bit of a butcher's once in a while, does it?

SHERRIL: Well, enjoy yourself, Sonia. I'm off.

(SHERRIL *exits.*)

SONIA: Honestly. Some people! They just don't know how
           to enjoy themselves!

           (She exits.)

TAKING IT FURTHER

Bible Background: Matthew 5:27–30

1. 'It's only a bit of fun.' Do you agree? Is there anything
   wrong with these types of show? Do you think that
   women see them differently from men?
2. 'Maybe there are some places we shouldn't escape to.'
   What do you think Sherril means by this? Do you think
   all daydreaming or fantasy is wrong?
3. 'There is more to a relationship than physical appearances.' What things do you look for in a relationship?
   What part does physical attraction play?
4. Read the Bible Background. What do you think Jesus
   means by this?

6. Total Commitment

Topic: Stickability and commitment.

Characters: TOM; BRIAN.

Setting: TOM and BRIAN meet in the pub. They sit at a table, drinking their beers.

Props/costume: Stools. Glasses (one part-filled). One packet of cigarettes. Lighter.

(TOM *is sitting with a drink in a pub. Enter* BRIAN.)

TOM: Hello. I didn't expect to see you here.

BRIAN: Why's that then?

TOM: I thought you did wossname on Tuesday nights – Nintendo.

BRIAN: Taikwondo.

TOM: Oh, right.

BRIAN: No, I gave that up. It just all got a bit too much. You know, the endless demands, the exhibitions, the exams, working your way through the different belts and all that. I really needed a change.

TOM: (*Pause*) You've only been doing it two weeks.

BRIAN: Yeah, but I packed a lot in. Anyway, I could see it weren't going nowhere. I mean, two whole sessions and we hadn't got much beyond grunting and wearing a pair of silly pyjamas. I thought by lesson two I should have been able to beat up ninja warriors and all that. I should be an expert.

TOM: Don't be daft; that takes years.

BRIAN: Does it?

TOM: Yeah – all those experts, they're all about 80, aren't they? All little old men who've spent about 30 years sitting meditating on the top of a mountain in Japan.

BRIAN: Well, you can stuff that. I'm not sitting on top of a cold mountain for anyone. Give you piles, that would. I learnt that when I was in the St John's Ambulance.

TOM: Yes, now how long were you with them?

BRIAN: Quite a long while.

TOM: Four weeks, wasn't it?

BRIAN: Well . . . three and a half. It was all a bit of a disappointment, really. All you ever did was deal with a load of ill people. And all that blood – yuck! I came over all faint. I never have been any good with injuries and all that.

TOM: What did you expect? It was the St John's Ambulance, after all. They're supposed to help injured people.

BRIAN: No one told me. I thought all you had to do was wear a uniform and you got into the football for free.

TOM: I suppose you have to pay now to see the Rovers.

BRIAN: Yeah . . . except I don't support the Rovers any more. Not since they were relegated. I support United.

TOM: *(Dismissively)* Typical.

BRIAN: What's that supposed to mean?

TOM: You just can't take it, can you? The moment things get difficult, you're out of it. When the going gets tough, Brian gets going.

BRIAN: That's not fair.

TOM: Well, can you think of one thing you've done – just one thing – where you've stuck it for more than a few weeks?

BRIAN: Of course I can. What about school? I went there for years.

TOM: Went there, but you never did anything. You failed every exam you ever took, because you couldn't be bothered to revise.

BRIAN: I'm not into all that revision stuff. I'm more the instinctive type.

TOM: Instinctively idle.

BRIAN: That is not true.

TOM: Well, tell me one thing you achieved at school, then.

BRIAN: *(Pause)* I built a chopping board in woodwork.

TOM: Yes. That's true. As I recall, though, it was about two-foot thick, on account of how it was supposed to be a fruit bowl, but you couldn't be bothered to hollow it out.

BRIAN: *(Hurt)* My mum treasured that chopping board.

TOM: Treasured it? It was so thick, she had to climb on a ladder to use the thing. She had to be rushed to hospital when she fell off it while dicing some carrots.

BRIAN: You're not being fair.

TOM: It's the truth, Brian, much as you might not like it. The moment things get tricky you disappear. It's true of jobs, training courses, even relationships. The longest relationship you ever had was that time when you got stuck with Janice in the lift. Sometimes you've just got to grit your teeth and keep going. If you really believe in something you have to see it through. I mean, look at me and Sandra. We have our rows, of course we do, but we're committed to each other. So we have to sort it out. We don't just run away.

BRIAN: I don't think you're being fair. I can stick at things. I have a lot of will-power.

TOM: Prove it.

BRIAN: OK. What do you want me to do?

TOM: I want you to give up the fags for a day.

BRIAN: *(Horrified)* A day!? What, a whole one?

TOM: Just 24 hours. That's all.

BRIAN: *(Determined)* All right. All right. I'll do it. I'll prove to you I can do it. You're wrong about me. I can see things through. I don't just change from one day to the next.

TOM: Right. Hand them over then.

BRIAN: No problem.

(He hands over a packet of cigarettes and a lighter.)

BRIAN: There you go.

TOM: Right. I'll see you tomorrow then.

(TOM finishes his drink and exits.)

BRIAN: No problem. Will-power. I'll show him. *(He pauses and then turns to speak to the bartender)* Fred – chuck us a packet of fags, mate.

TAKING IT FURTHER

Bible Background: Hebrews 12:1–3

1. Have you ever wanted to give something up, but kept going with it? What was the result?
2. 'If you really believe in something, you have to see it through.' What things might Tom be talking about?
3. Read the Bible Background. What kinds of thing might make a Christian want to give up 'running the race'?
4. How can we help others who are struggling to keep going?

7. Change Your Life

Topic: Physical appearance and self-image.

Characters: DOCTOR; JANE.

Setting: A doctor's surgery. The DOCTOR sits behind a desk or table. JANE sits the other side of it.

Props/costume: Display cards of noses. Desk/table. Two chairs. White coat for the DOCTOR.

(The DOCTOR is sitting behind a desk. Enter JANE.)

DOCTOR: Welcome, welcome – now what can I do for you?

JANE: I've come about the advert.

DOCTOR: What – remove unsightly nasal hair without pain or discomfort?

JANE: Er . . . no. The one about, you know, face-lifts and all that.

DOCTOR: Ah, cosmetic surgery. I thought you wouldn't need the nasal hair. I mean I had a quick look when you came in and I didn't see anything dangling around. Mind you, I could always have a quick go, just to be on the safe side.

JANE: No thank you very much.

DOCTOR: Suit yourself. Now, what appears to be the problem?

JANE: It's my nose. I can't stand my nose.

DOCTOR: What's wrong with it?

JANE: It's the wrong shape. Look at the end – it goes up when it should carry straight on. I hate it.

DOCTOR: Well, we do a wide range of noses.

(He picks up a range of display cards and shows them to JANE.)

DOCTOR: There's the Cleopatra . . . the Classic Roman . . . and the Rolls-Royce of noses, the Rhino Pro.

JANE: Amazing.

DOCTOR: Yes, that's obviously more expensive, because of the extra materials.

JANE: Well, I don't fancy any of those. Can't you give me something a bit different?

DOCTOR: I can give you the Boxer's Special.

JANE: What's one of those?

DOCTOR: I just hit you in the face with a hammer.

JANE: Well, perhaps I'll have my cheeks done instead. I'd like more definition, higher cheekbones, you know. I want to look dramatic and interesting.

DOCTOR: Couldn't you just use make-up?

JANE: Make-up doesn't change anything. Make-up is just the surface. I want a new me.

DOCTOR: Er . . . this is cosmetic surgery we're talking about here. It doesn't really *change* you. All it does is, well, alter the packaging.

JANE: You don't understand. You don't have to live looking like me.

DOCTOR: I think you may be getting things a bit out of proportion. I mean, we're not talking Quasimodo here. All right, maybe there's a bit of structural alteration we could do – a nip here, a tuck there – but there's nothing basically wrong, is there?

JANE: *(Ignoring him)* Perhaps I'll have some liposuction. Get rid of this excess fat. That's it – take the fat from here *(indicating stomach)* and use some of it up here *(pointing to cheeks)* to sort of build it up. We could use any that's left over to alter my nose.

DOCTOR: Why do you want this?

JANE: Look at me! I hate the way I look. If only I could look different, everything would be changed. If I looked glamorous . . . beautiful . . . I would be happy. I would be content.

DOCTOR: I'm sorry. I don't think there's anything I can do for you.

JANE: But I'm prepared to pay.

DOCTOR: No, it's not that. It's just what you want changed can't be changed. Not by me, at any rate. I can make you look different, but I can't make you like yourself.

JANE: No, you're right. I'm silly looking for satisfaction here.

DOCTOR: That's right.

JANE: There's a sale on at Harvey Nicholls – I'll go there instead!

(JANE exits.)

TAKING IT FURTHER

Bible Background: Psalm 139:1–24

1. 'I hate the way I look.' Do you think how you look matters?
2. 'If I looked glamorous I would be happy.' Why do people think this way?
3. Do you think our society is obsessed with appearance?

4. Read the Bible Background. What does this say about the way in which we ought to regard ourselves?
5. Do you think it matters to God how you look? Do you think God cares about appearances?

8. Can Eat, Should Eat?

Topic: Gluttony.

Characters: JEAN *(French chef)*; ERIC.

Setting: A TV cookery programme. JEAN stands behind a table or bench on which is an array of cooking implements and some vegetables.

Props/costume: Table or bench. Cooking implements. Some vegetables, notably a parsnip. If you can't get a parsnip, the gag works just as well with a carrot. Or, frankly, any other root vegetable. ERIC has a can of beans hidden either in a pocket or in a plain shopping bag which he brings on stage with him. JEAN wears a chef's hat and a white apron.

> (*Enter* JEAN. *He is a typical television chef, albeit with an outrageous French accent.*)

JEAN: 'Allo, my leetle gherkins, and welcome to anuzzer edition of *Could Cook, Don't Cook*, ze top TV cookery programme, in which we take a complete idiot and laugh at him as his soufflé collapses. I am, of course, ze famous chef Jean-Paul Blancmange and our contestant tonight is Eric Spud from Cleethorpes. Bonjour, Eric!

> (*Enter* ERIC.)

ERIC: Hello, Jean. *(Throughout this sketch he pronounces it as 'Gene')*

JEAN: *(Correcting him with the French version)* Jean.

ERIC: Sorry?

JEAN: Jean – my name is Jean. Jean-Paul. Now what kind of food do you like?

ERIC: *(Ignoring him)* Well, Jean, I like pretty sophisticated stuff, you know.

JEAN: You do?

ERIC: Oh yes. I don't just have beans on toast, you know. I have beans on toast with some cheese sprinkled on the top.

JEAN: *(Unimpressed)* Astonishing.

ERIC: And then, for afters, we frequently have *(pauses impressively)* toffee yoghurt!

JEAN: *(Dripping with sarcasm)* Well, you are certainly ze little gourmet, *non*?

ERIC: I like to think so.

JEAN: But for zis show, my little *pomme de terre*, we are going to create a gastronomique extravaganza, a fantastic feast, how you say, 'a real gutbuster'.

ERIC: Super. Will there be beans in it?

JEAN: *Non.*

ERIC: Oh.

JEAN: *(To audience)* For zis feast we will cook three ducks, all stuffed wiz a mixture of truffles and ze finest armagnac brandy. To accompany zis we will 'ave *pâté de foie gras* gently cooked wiz rare and expensive wild mushrooms. All washed down wiz a bottle of 1921 Chablis.

ERIC: *(Pause)* No beans, then.

JEAN: *Non.* Zis is a gourmet feast.

ERIC: Er Jean –

JEAN: *(Correcting him)* Jean.

ERIC: *(Still doing it wrong)* Jean. I was just wondering . . . It's rather a lot, isn't it? I mean, all that for two people. Isn't that a bit piggy?

JEAN: 'A bit piggy?' Zis is gourmet food!

ERIC: Only it's just, well, I was watching this documentary before I come here tonight, and it was all about these people in Africa. And they haven't got anything to eat at all. Not even beans. I dunno, it seems a bit wrong to be stuffing ourselves.

JEAN: Oh, don't be such a silly-billy! What on earth can we do about them? I mean we can't send zem a piece of duck.

ERIC: No, but, I dunno. Maybe we should think a bit more about how much we eat.

JEAN: Oh Eric, my little blancmange. It makes no difference to zem, what I eat here. Now, let us get cooking . . . *(Taking a parsnip from the table)* First, we take our parsnip and –

ERIC: *(Interrupting)* Yes, but don't you think that we have some kind of responsibility here?

(There is no response.)

ERIC: Well?

JEAN: I am just thinking where to place this parsnip. *(Making an effort)* Look, if I don't eat, will zat help zem?

ERIC: No, but –

JEAN: And if I throw all this away, will zat help zem?

ERIC: Of course not –

JEAN: So zere we are. It makes no difference.

ERIC: But is it right? I mean, maybe we should have thought about it before buying the meal. While we were in the supermarket.

JEAN: Look, I understand your anxiety, my little chicken nugget, but we must eat. We must live. And is it wrong to eat nice things?

ERIC: No. You're right. We should eat nice things.

JEAN: Zat's ze spirit.

ERIC: Let's cook the meal.

JEAN: *Absolument*!

ERIC: Roast duck!

JEAN: *(Excitedly) Très bon*!

ERIC: Truffles!

JEAN: *(More excitedly) Très, très bon*!

ERIC: Wild mushrooms!

JEAN: *(Very excitedly) Très, très, très bon*!

ERIC: *(Producing the can of beans)* And beans!

JEAN: *(Pause)* I give up.

(JEAN exits in disgust.)

TAKING IT FURTHER

Bible Background: Proverbs 23:1–3

1. Why does Eric feel guilty?
2. Is it wrong to eat nice things?
3. What kinds of factor should influence our food-buying?
4. In what ways can our food consumption affect other people?
5. How much should we pay for a meal? What do you think is reasonable?
6. Is there any way Eric could have enjoyed his food and helped other people?

9. The Disappointed

Topic: Disappointment.

Characters: KEVIN; KAREN; JULIE.

Setting: This takes place on a plain stage. The actors stand facing the audience and speak directly to them. It is as if we are eavesdropping on the characters' private thoughts and feelings. Although the characters refer to each other, they do not communicate. Each is in their own little world.

Props/costume: None.

(KAREN, KEVIN and JULIE stand facing the front.)

KAREN: I mean, it wasn't like I didn't work or anything. I did all the revision. I felt really prepared for the exam as well. I don't know what more I could have done. It's not like I meant to fail.

KEVIN: Every Saturday it's the same. You look forward all week to the match. You think, 'This is the week! This week it will be different.'

JULIE: I like Kevin. And I think he likes me. I know you shouldn't build up your hopes – my mum says I'm always dreaming! But I think he really likes me. I just don't know what to do. I've tried to talk to Karen about it, but she's not been the same since the exam. Got her own problems, I suppose.

KAREN: I worked really hard. I did. That's what makes it so

awful in a way. I thought I'd done really well. I'd written a good piece on 'Shakespeare's Use of Power Tools in *Othello*' and I was really pleased with my essay on 'The Image of the Aardvark in the Short Stories of D.H. Lawrence'. So when I saw the result . . . it was a kick in the teeth.

KEVIN: Saturday morning was great. It always is. You think, today it's going to happen. Today I'm going to make the team. Start out on the subs bench, but when Darren is injured in the first minute I'm called on and we go on to win the match 19–0. *(Pause)* Of which I score 18. And the manager turns to me and says, 'I've misjudged you, son. I now realise that you are a huge talent, and Darren has all the footballing ability of a large fencepost.'

JULIE: Anyway, I knew I was looking good, because I'd made myself up really well. I'd got this new perfume from Boots – it's called *(pouting)* 'Voluptuous'. I knew I was pretty well irresistible. So, I had high hopes that tonight he would notice me.

KAREN: I had such high hopes. I thought it would be an 'A'. A 'B' at worst. But a 'D'! What went wrong? It's the story of my life – nothing ever goes as planned. I don't know what they'll say. Maybe they'll be angry. Dad might shout. He always shouts when he's disappointed. I don't. I clam up. Dig a hole and crawl in. Decided not to go to the party. I mean, everyone knows, don't they?

KEVIN: I got to the playing ground in plenty of time, toyed with the idea of ambushing Darren in the car park and beating him up before the game – but decided that wasn't very sporting. Went into the changing room – everyone's there. Everybody's buzzing. And there's the team sheet up on the wall and there's my name! *(Pause)* Third substitute. Just behind Tommy, the one-man defensive error, and Dave, the goalie with two left hands. *(Bitterly)* Not even first choice. And I thought this was going to be my week . . .

JULIE: And then, when he walked in, I was so excited. This was my chance. This week he would notice me. I saw from the start that he needed comforting and I was thinking, 'He's suffering!' *(Pause, then excitedly)* GREAT! *(Calming down)* Not that I want him to suffer, but it's like in the films, isn't it, you know, like he's got a tragic secret that he's hiding from the world. Maybe he's nursing a broken heart and is just looking for the right woman – i.e. me. Or maybe he's lost both legs in a bizarre bungee-jump-related accident and he needs someone to nurse him through his suffering – *(Pause)* i.e. me again.

KAREN: I was so excited. So hopeful. That's all changed now.

KEVIN: Five minutes. That's all. Five minutes from the end I get on to play.

JULIE: Of course, he hadn't lost both legs because he walked in to the party, but you know what I mean.

KAREN: If I can't pass that exam, what hope for all the others? I can see what life's going to be like, you know. One long succession of disappointments.

KEVIN: Hardly had a touch of the ball. Went to a party in the evening. Left early. Couldn't bear to be with anyone. *(Pause)* It wouldn't be so bad if I didn't love playing football so much.

JULIE: I went to check everything looked OK, add another dollop of 'Voluptuous', and when I came out . . . he was gone. I asked after him and they said he was in a mood and had just left. All that waiting. All for nothing. I phoned Karen, but she didn't answer.

KAREN: The phone rang. I didn't answer it.

KEVIN: I just didn't feel like partying.

TAKING IT FURTHER

Bible Background: 2 Corinthians 1:3–5

1. Have you ever suffered a major disappointment? What was it?
2. 'I clam up. Dig a hole and crawl in.' How do you react to disappointment?
3. How can we help people like Kevin, Julie and Karen? What would make things better?
4. Read the Bible Background. What does Paul say about offering comfort?

10. Happy Feet

Topic: Advertising.

Characters: CUSTOMER; ASSISTANT.

Setting: a trendy shoeshop – one of those that masquerades as a sports shop. The ASSISTANT stands behind a table that serves as the sales counter. If you want to add to the effect you could always have a few shoeboxes open on the table.

Props/costume: Table. Torn-out magazine advert. Shoeboxes (optional). The CUSTOMER should wear the biggest and most garish shoes you can find. If you can find an old pair of trainers and paint them some luminous colour it will work a treat.

CUSTOMER: Hello.

ASSISTANT: Hello, sir, what can we do for you?

CUSTOMER: Well, it's about this pair of shoes I bought the other day.

ASSISTANT: Oh yes, the Trailblazing Hyper-Comfy-Sole Max.

CUSTOMER: Well, they don't do what the adverts said they would.

ASSISTANT: What's the matter – aren't they waterproof?

CUSTOMER: Yes.

ASSISTANT: Comfortable?

CUSTOMER: Yes, very.

ASSISTANT: Soothing to your feet with their foot-massage textured sole?

CUSTOMER: Yes, that's all very nice.

ASSISTANT: Ah. It's the . . . um . . . problem, then, isn't it?

CUSTOMER: Sorry?

ASSISTANT: *(Whispers)* The odour. You're having a problem with the Stink-No-More inner sole. I thought when you walked in that things weren't right.

CUSTOMER: No it's not that –

ASSISTANT: Only I could see several people start to gag as you walked by.

CUSTOMER: No, it's just –

ASSISTANT: And there's a dog over there that fainted when you got the shoes out of the box.

CUSTOMER: It's not that.

ASSISTANT: Are you sure?

CUSTOMER: I do not have smelly feet.

ASSISTANT: *(Pause)* Well, you could have fooled me.

CUSTOMER: Will you stop going on about it!

ASSISTANT: Well, what is it then?

CUSTOMER: It's this advert.

(CUSTOMER produces a torn-out page from a magazine.)

ASSISTANT: What's the matter?

CUSTOMER: This says 'The Trailblazing Hyper-Comfy-Sole Max – The shoe that sets you free.'

ASSISTANT: And?

CUSTOMER: Well, it hasn't.

ASSISTANT: Hasn't what?

CUSTOMER: It hasn't set me free. I thought that if I bought this shoe I would be given a new lease of life. I thought I could spend the rest of my life bounding up mountainsides free from all cares and responsibilities. 'Great!', I thought. 'No more credit card debt! No more work on Monday morning! No more ties!' But it hasn't done any of that.

ASSISTANT: But it's just an advert . . .

CUSTOMER: And look at the bloke wearing them as well! Fit, tanned, young . . . I don't look anything like him.

ASSISTANT: I think you might be taking things a little too literally, sir. I mean, it doesn't really mean 'set you free'. It just means, er . . . 'You might feel quite good in them.'

CUSTOMER: Why didn't they say that?

ASSISTANT: Well, it's not very much of a slogan, is it? 'The Trailblazing Hyper-Comfy-Sole Max – You might feel quite good in them.'

CUSTOMER: It's the same with all these adverts. I used my credit card because they said it 'took the pain out of paying'. Now I've got credit card debts the size of a small South American country. I repainted my room with 'Sunburst – the Colour of Sunshine' and it rained for the next three days. I wear all the right labels, splash myself with the latest after-shaves and it doesn't solve the problem.

ASSISTANT: Well, maybe you should try pouring the after-shave into your shoes.

CUSTOMER: Not that problem! Freedom. Happiness. Contentment.

ASSISTANT: Look, advertising doesn't work that way. It's just trying to give you a feeling. It's about linking the product with an emotion. That's the way it works. It's not reality. I mean, when you see cowboys riding through Marlboro Country, you don't see them tether their horse outside the lung cancer units, do you? The world of advertising is a perfect world, sir. Where everyone is beautiful and happy.

CUSTOMER: So these won't really set me free, then? They won't make me happy? Or fulfilled?

ASSISTANT: I'm afraid not.

CUSTOMER: Oh.

ASSISTANT: They might make you smell better, though.

TAKING IT FURTHER

Bible Background: Proverbs 17:24

1. Do you watch the adverts? Which is your favourite? Why?
2. Do you believe what they tell you? Which ones are making genuine claims?
3. Someone once defined advertising as 'The truth, told well'. Do you agree?
4. 'It's just trying to give you a feeling. It's about linking the product with an emotion.' Do you agree with this? Can you think of any examples?
5. How can we distinguish between what is good and bad in any advert?

11. Reading Between the Lines

Topic: Gossip.

Characters: HARRY; JANE; BRIAN; SUSAN; LOUISA.

Setting: The action takes place on a plain stage and unfolds in a series of dialogues. As one character leaves, another enters to take their place. The cast have paper cups of coffee as if they have met at the coffee bar. Since one of these cups has to be chucked over HARRY, it is best to fill them with water rather than real coffee. I take no responsibility for your dry-cleaning bill!

Props/costume: Paper coffee cups.

(Enter HARRY *and* JANE.*)*

JANE: Are you all right?

HARRY: It's Linford. He's dead.

JANE: Oh, Harry, I'm so sorry . . . Who was Linford?

HARRY: My tortoise.

JANE: Of course.

HARRY: I went to wake him up from his hibernation and he . . . he'd gone. You know, when something like this happens you wonder, could I have taken more care of him? Should I have given him better lettuce? Did he need more straw? *(Starting to get emotional)* And I never once took him for walkies!

JANE: *(Comforting him)* There, there, let it all out . . .

(HARRY *exits. Enter* BRIAN. *They are drinking coffee.*)

BRIAN: How's Harry?

JANE: Not good, I'm afraid. His tortoise has died.

BRIAN: Oh, that's tough.

JANE: Yeah. It's funny –

BRIAN: What?

JANE: Well, he kept going on about how he wished he'd behaved better. It was almost as if he was guilty or something . . . He said how he hadn't given the creature enough lettuce. I don't know. We shouldn't read too much into it.

BRIAN: Well, they do say that people are at their most honest at moments of stress.

JANE: Perhaps I'm just imagining things. But he was really cut up about it.

(JANE *exits. Enter* SUSAN *with cup of coffee.*)

BRIAN: I met Jane down the pub.

SUSAN: Oh yes?

BRIAN: Well, you'll never guess what she told me. Harry killed his tortoise.

SUSAN: Harry?

BRIAN: Apparently. Starved him of lettuce and then, after he died . . . No, I can't say.

SUSAN: What?

BRIAN: It's too horrible.

SUSAN: Go on, you can tell me.

BRIAN: He cut it up.

SUSAN: *(Horrified)* No!

BRIAN: That's what she said. With an axe.

SUSAN: Oh . . . that's appalling. Surely the RSPCA would do something?

BRIAN: They didn't know. I only found out from the hints that Jane dropped. You know, reading between the lines . . .

(BRIAN exits. Enter LOUISA with cup of coffee.)

LOUISA: I can't believe it!

SUSAN: Well, I'm only saying what I heard. He ate his tortoise.

LOUISA: But Harry – I thought he was vegetarian.

SUSAN: Still waters run deep, you know. On the surface butter wouldn't melt in his mouth, but beneath it all there lurks the mind of a depraved, tortoise-hating axe-murderer. He's the Hannibal Lecter of the reptilian world.

LOUISA: And to think I'm supposed to be going to the zoo with him tomorrow. He's probably just scouting for more victims.

SUSAN: Well, you know, I'm not one to gossip, but I thought you ought to know. What with you two being friends and all that.

LOUISA: Not any more. Not now I know the truth.

(SUSAN exits. Enter HARRY.)

HARRY: Hi! Sorry I'm a bit late.

(LOUISA throws her coffee over him.)

LOUISA: Tortoise murderer!

(She exits. HARRY looks bewildered.)

HARRY: Was it something I said?

TAKING IT FURTHER

Bible Background: Ephesians 4:29–32; Proverbs 16:28

1. How did all this get out of hand? Where do you think the problem lies?
2. We all like a good gossip – but why?
3. Can gossip be harmful? Think of any examples you know.
4. How should we react when people start telling us the latest gossip?
5. Read the Bible Background. Why does Paul warn against such talk?

12. The Monk in Flat 24

Topic: Ghosts. The supernatural.

Characters: KIMBERLEY; JADE.

Setting: A pub. KIMBERLEY and JADE are sitting at a table with their drinks.

Props/costume: Some drinks. A small table and two chairs.

(KIMBERLEY and JADE are sitting in a pub.)

KIMBERLEY: I had this weird experience the other night. It was midnight. I was lying in bed in the total darkness. The whole room went cold. It was like feeling an icy hand all over me.

JADE: Your Vernon getting frisky, was he?

KIMBERLEY: No, no, it wasn't Vernon. I mean, granted, he gives me a horrible creepy sensation, but this was a totally different horrible creepy sensation. Then there was a huge thumping noise.

JADE: Probably the plumbing.

KIMBERLEY: No, it shook the whole room. And I sat up and there was this figure there! A hooded figure, like a monk or a nun.

JADE: What was a monk doing in your bedroom at midnight?

KIMBERLEY: It wasn't a real monk, you idiot. It was a ghost.

JADE: A ghost?

KIMBERLEY: Yes. Obviously, at one time our house has been inhabited by a monk. And he now haunts the place.

JADE: *(Pause)* You live in a council flat. *(Pause)* Built in 1963.

KIMBERLEY: Well, maybe the flats were built on the site of a monastery. And now this poor, lost spirit haunts the place, searching endlessly for his monastery, and finding only a load of council flats.

JADE: Poor soul. I mean, it's bad enough being dead without having to spend time in your flat.

KIMBERLEY: What's that supposed to mean?

JADE: Well, it's hardly the most hygienic place in the world, is it? Mind you, if he is a medieval monk he probably feels at home. After all, he could catch the bubonic plague in your kitchen.

KIMBERLEY: But I haven't told you the weirdest bit. *(Whispering)* He spoke to me!

JADE: He did?

KIMBERLEY: Yes.

JADE: What did he say? Was it, 'Let me out of this crummy flat?'

KIMBERLEY: You're not taking this seriously, are you?

JADE: Sorry. Go on.

KIMBERLEY: No, this unearthly voice said, 'I can't get up.'

JADE: Is that it?

KIMBERLEY: Well, don't you see? 'I can't get up.' He is tied down. He is trapped for all eternity. It is a message from the spirit world.

JADE: Yeah, I get those.

KIMBERLEY: You do?

JADE: Yeah. Of course it depends on how many spirits I've had. Gin normally does the trick.

KIMBERLEY: You can scoff. But I believe he had a message for me.

JADE: Well, I think you should leave well alone. Nothing good ever comes of that sort of thing.

KIMBERLEY: You're just a sceptic.

JADE: No, I'm not. That's the point. I just think that there are things we're not supposed to know.

KIMBERLEY: Oh, don't be such a wet blanket. My Auntie Maureen was a medium.

JADE: She never was. Your Auntie Maureen was extra extra large. And that was when she breathed in.

KIMBERLEY: No, she could intercede between the spirit world and here. She always said that Vernon had an 'aura'.

JADE: There's no denying that. I've noticed the ways the flies buzz around him.

KIMBERLEY: She claimed that the spirits would guide us. She said it was a comfort.

JADE: I can't see why. I would hope that my dead relatives have got better things to do than hang about waiting for your Auntie Maureen to call them up. No, I reckon that either these people are cons, using simple tricks to get people's money, or –

KIMBERLEY: Or what?

JADE: Or they are dabbling with things that we should leave alone. There are things we should not delve into. Namely the spirit world and your laundry basket. It's not just harmless fun.

KIMBERLEY: Well, I have to admit that manifestation gave me a bit of a fright. I said so to my Vernon the next morning as he got up from the floor.

JADE: What was he doing down there?

KIMBERLEY: Ah, that's the spooky thing, you see. I think he

must have been affected by this ghost. 'Cos Vern said he came in from the pub and couldn't find the bed. And the carpet was all pulled up by the door. So maybe the ghost moved the bed in the night.

JADE: *(Thinks)* You keep your dressing-gown hanging on the back of the door, don't you?

KIMBERLEY: Yeah. Why?

JADE: Well, it's just a theory, you know, but you don't think that what might have happened is this:
             Vernon gets back from the pub and opens the door. The temperature drops. Vernon falls over the carpet. You wake up and see your dressing-gown on the back of the door. Vern, lying on the floor, says 'I can't get up.' You decide the whole thing is a psychic phenomenon.

             (There is a pause.)

KIMBERLEY: That is the most stupid thing I have ever heard in my life.

JADE: Yeah. Of course.

KIMBERLEY: I mean, you'd have to be an idiot to believe in all that.

TAKING IT FURTHER

Bible Background: Deuteronomy 18:9–11

1. What do people mean when they talk about 'the spirit world'?
2. Why might people find it 'comforting' to talk to spirits?
3. 'Either it's a con, or they are dabbling with things that we should leave alone.' Do you agree?

4. Why do you think it might be dangerous to pursue these interests? Are there areas we should leave alone?
5. 'I just think that there are things we're not supposed to know.' Do you agree?

13. On the Bench

Topic: Homelessness.

Characters: ONE – a businessman or woman; TWO – a shopper; THREE – a homeless person.

Setting: Park bench.

Props/costume: Bench. It's not necessary to go overboard with costume; just get one or two items to suggest the character. The businessman could be dressed in a suit and tie. The shopper could be male or female but should be carrying two large carrier bags, ideally from famous clothes shops. The homeless person could wear a large, scruffy coat and worn-out shoes.

> *(Three people are sitting on a park bench. They talk directly to the audience, as if being interviewed or speaking to camera.)*

ONE: Let's knock on the door and ask for Mr Reality, shall we? Nobody in this country needs to be homeless these days. Councils have a duty to rehouse people. There are laws. The only reason people are out on the streets is because they're drunk or stupid or both. That's the truth.

TWO: It's the youngsters I feel sorry for. I see them sitting in the tube stations and in the shop doors and I wonder how they got there. They always have those signs – 'Hungry and Homeless – Please Help.' And I want to help. I just don't know what to do for the best.

THREE: You've got to learn how to survive on the street. And you have to learn quick. There are places to go and things to do. There are techniques you can learn. I'm good at it. I've been living here for years. This is my bench.

ONE: The thing is that we've turned into this 'nanny' state. I honestly think that there is too much provision for failure and idleness. Look, I'm not being cruel, I'm being realistic. I've been unemployed. I've had my fair share of problems. But I never gave in. I kept going and I pulled myself out of it.

TWO: The other day I noticed a girl begging. And I gave her some money. Then, when I was coming back from the shops, I saw her again. She was talking to a friend, or her sister or something. They were, I don't know, discussing things. Organised. I don't know what was going on. Maybe it was some kind of, what's it called, 'ring'. A begging ring, I think they call it. I don't know. Was I wrong to give her money?

THREE: First, find your spot. I choose this place because just over there are some government buildings. And that means closed-circuit TV, which means security. You're less likely to get your bags nicked if there's a camera nearby. Never sleep in a box. Boxes are for mugs. You get trouble near you and you can't escape. No – sleeping here, I can be up and off at the first sign of any trouble. No fuss.

ONE: Look, I'm not callous. I want to help the needy. But I want to help the genuine ones. Not the scroungers or the idle. What we need is a new system. That's why I don't give to charities. You give to a charity and it merely perpetuates the problem. It doesn't matter whether you're talking about Africa or Acton, if people are constantly receiving hand-outs, then they are never going to stand on their own two feet, are they?

TWO: Then you get people asking you for money and you know that they're going to blow it on drink. You just know it. Oh, they spin you some story about a ticket or something. But if I gave them anything they'd be down the off-licence quicker than you can say Bulmer's Cider.

THREE: Of course you drink. Listen – you're cold. You're hurting. Everyone you meet looks down at you. Drink dulls the pain. I don't binge. But I have my moments, like everyone. Only mugs get really drunk. If you're drunk, you're defenceless. The last time I got drunk someone nicked my boots. And they were good boots as well. So I never get drunk any more. I've learnt.

ONE: What is needed is good, low-cost accommodation. That's the root cause. And we're not going to change that with a few sticking plasters and some free sandwiches. The way to help is to help long-term.

TWO: I think to myself, 'What would Jesus do?' But that's really difficult, isn't it? Because he'd probably rustle up a three-course meal out of a can of pilchards and a few slices of Mother's Pride. I try to give to a few charities. You know, that way I feel like I'm doing something, and that I will really be helping the problem. It's just when you see them, lying in the street . . .

THREE: You don't have friends on the streets. There are people you run into, people you know. But I left my friends behind years ago. My boots, my sleeping-bag

– these are the only friends I know. Take care of them and they'll take care of you.

ONE: We have to trust people to get on with it. Let them sort themselves out.

TWO: I want to know who to trust with my concern. I don't want to be fooled. I want to help.

THREE: Trust no one. That's the key. Look after number one. No one cares whether you live or die. It's up to you.

TAKING IT FURTHER

Bible Background: Isaiah 58:6–10

1. Why do you think people are homeless? What do we mean by 'homelessness'?
2. 'If people receive hand-outs they're never going to stand on their own two feet.' What do you think the character means by this? Is it true?
3. What do you think Jesus would do about the problem? What does that teach us?
4. 'I want to help. I just don't know what to do for the best.' How can we best get involved?

14. Written in the Stars . . .

Topic: Horoscopes.

Characters: DISCO MAN – hopelessly stuck in the seventies (think Austin Powers but with an Afro); SHARON; GERALDINE; PENNY.

Setting: Dance floor. For modern authenticity this should be set in a club, but if you fancy a touch of nostalgia, you could go for a kitsch seventies disco look. If you can get hold of a mirrorball, so much the better.

Props/costume: Three handbags. Medallion. One pair of sunglasses. Maybe some disco music in the background.

> *(Three girls are dancing around their handbags. Enter DISCO MAN. He is your classic seventies disco dude, complete with medallion and sunglasses. He boogies over to SHARON.)*

DISCO MAN: Hi.

SHARON: Hi.

DISCO MAN: Sagittarius, right?

SHARON: Sorry?

DISCO MAN: Sagittarius. Your star sign. I can always tell. Sagittarians are so elegant and self-assured.

SHARON: Are we?

DISCO MAN: Oh yeah. And they're beautiful movers.

SHARON: But I'm Libra.

DISCO MAN: *(Recovering quickly)* And Librans as well. They're the same.

SHARON: Oh. I thought all the star sign things were different. What are you, then?

DISCO MAN: Aries. The ram.

SHARON: Do you believe all that, then?

DISCO MAN: Oh yeah. Our lives are determined by the stars, baby. It's fate, bringing us together. Two lives picked out by the measureless firmament to dwell for ever in perfect love and harmony.

SHARON: *(Ignoring him completely)* Only I think it's a load of codswallop.

DISCO MAN: *(Hurriedly)* Yeah, yeah, me too.

SHARON: My mum reads her horoscope every day. I s'pose it's harmless fun. That and the tarot. And the palm-reading. Just a laugh. Mind you, I was a bit worried when she started disembowelling a chicken and reading the entrails. See you . . .

(SHARON dances off. DISCO MAN dances across to GERALDINE.)

DISCO MAN: Hi.

GERALDINE: Hi.

DISCO MAN: Sagittarius, right?

GERALDINE: No, Geraldine.

DISCO MAN: No – your star sign.

GERALDINE: Oh no. I'm Pisces. The fish. We're lively and intelligent and optometric.

DISCO MAN: Optimistic.

GERALDINE: That as well. I think horoscopes are great, aren't they?

DISCO MAN: Oh yeah, especially when they bring –

GERALDINE: *(Interrupting him)* My lucky number is seven

and my lucky stone is gall. Do you know, it's incredible, isn't it? My horoscope today said, 'You will go out. Money may be involved. Something may happen.'

DISCO MAN: Incredible.

GERALDINE: That's what I love about horoscopes. They're always so accurate.

DISCO MAN: And did it mention a tall, dark stranger?

GERALDINE: Yeah, it did actually.

DISCO MAN: Great.

GERALDINE: That's him over there. See you.

(GERALDINE *dances off.* DISCO MAN *dances over to* PENNY.)

DISCO MAN: Hi.

PENNY: Hi.

DISCO MAN: Sagittarius, right?

PENNY: No. Baptist, actually.

DISCO MAN: No, your star sign. Sagittarius. I can always tell. Because Sagittarians are so elegant and self-assured. What do you think I am?

PENNY: A prat?

DISCO MAN: No, my star sign.

PENNY: Look, I don't know and I don't care. I try to keep away from all that rubbish.

DISCO MAN: You don't believe it, then?

PENNY: Believe it? No. I don't believe my life is controlled by the stars or when I was born. I believe in freedom. I believe in choice. I believe that anyone who dabbles in that kind of area is playing with forces he doesn't understand.

DISCO MAN: *(Pause)* It was only a harmless chat-up line.

PENNY: There is nothing harmless about the occult, mate.

DISCO MAN: Horoscopes aren't the occult! Horoscopes are just a bit of fun in your daily paper. The occult is, well, seances and poltergeists and all that stuff. Horoscopes – they're just . . . well, predicting what will happen. Like, you and me . . .

PENNY: Let me give you a prediction. I reckon in about five seconds you are going to feel very silly.

DISCO MAN: No chance of that, sweetheart.

(DISCO MAN starts to dance in what he thinks is an impressive way. PENNY dances off without his noticing.)

DISCO MAN: I'm Aries, baby. Cool and sophisticated. That's why they call me the lurve machine . . .

(He turns round and realises he is dancing on his own.)

DISCO MAN: Oh. *(Calling after her)* Hey! Wait a minute, how did you know that was going to happen?

(Exits.)

TAKING IT FURTHER

Bible Background: Isaiah 8:19–20

1. Why do people read their horoscopes?
2. If horoscopes work, how come Mystic Meg isn't rich?
3. 'Just a bit of harmless fun.' Do you think this is true?
4. 'Anyone who dabbles in that kind of area is playing with forces he doesn't understand.' Is she going a bit over the top?

15. Here I Am, Lord, Send Someone Else!

Topic: Involvement in church.

Characters: ONE; TWO; THREE; FOUR; FIVE.

Setting: Bare stage. The cast stand in a line across the stage, each speaking into their mobile phones.

Props/costume: Five mobile phones.

> *(The characters in this sketch line up across the stage.)*

ONE: Look, I'm studying for my A-Levels, right? *(Emphasising)* A-Levels. Probably the most important exams in my life. So I haven't got the time to do anything in the church. Yes, I know they're two years away yet . . . Yes, yes, I am only doing applied Play-doh modelling, but it still demands a lot of me, you know. No. Sorry.

TWO: Ah, well, the thing is, I'd love to help out, really I would. But I've got this Saturday job. *(Reacting to someone correcting him/her)* Sorry? It's on a Sunday? That's why they call it Sunday school? Yeah, but what time is it? Oh come on, I'm not even conscious by 11 a.m. And anyway, there would be stuff like preparation, wouldn't there? I've never been very good at preparing things. I had to prepare a meal once and it was a disaster.

THREE: *(Nodding, as if in agreement)* Right . . . right . . . right . . . right . . . right . . . right . . . yeah . . . I see . . . right . . . *(Pause)* Nah. Sorry, mate.

FOUR: Yes, but I'm not trained. I mean, I should do a lot more study before taking on anything like that. Well, I've done Old Testament History and New Testament Greek and Latin and Hermeneutics and Systematic Theology, but there are a lot of other courses that I'd need. Pastoral care, for example. Situational ethics. No, I really think we have to be theologically prepared before taking on these big tasks. Well, you might think that serving the coffee is simple, but, to me, it's a complex ministry and I don't think I'm up to it.

FIVE: Look, I'm sorry, but I'm not gifted in that area. You know, some are born to be preachers, some teachers, some prophets, etc etc. And I just don't have the gift of interior woodwork. Sorry.

ONE: And anyway, I'm not sure I'm ready for this kind of responsibility. I mean, I'm only 16. It's too young. I don't care if Elisha was only 14 – he was a prophet in Israel. I am a teenager in Wigan. Anyway, there's a big difference between raising the dead and defeating the Aramaean army and helping out at the youth club. I think even he would have run away from that one.

TWO: Also, I don't know the Bible well enough. Well, I know that this would teach me, but then I'd have to read it, wouldn't I? And I've never been good at reading. I had to read a recipe once. It was a disaster.

THREE: *(Nodding)* Right . . . right . . . right . . . right . . . right . . . right . . . yeah . . . OK . . . *(Pause)* Nah.

FOUR: Then there's Christology, Eschatology, Missiology, Biology and Ecology, Coffee-ology, Tea-ology,

Sugar-ology. You need training for this kind of thing.

FIVE: I've prayed for it, believe me. I've spent hours on my knees pleading with the Lord to give me the gifts of redecoration and allied DIY skills, but so far he hasn't seen fit, in his eternal wisdom, to answer my prayers. I just don't have a calling to woodwork.

ONE: Yes, yes, I do understand. Of course you need people. But I'm just not ready for the responsibility.

TWO: It's not that I don't want to. I just can't. It would be a disaster.

THREE: *(Nodding and getting increasingly enthusiastic)* Yeah . . . yeah . . . right . . . yeah . . . *(Pause)* Nah.

FOUR: I'm not trained. Give me a few more years' study, then I might be ready to pour the milk. Under proper supervision, of course.

FIVE: *(Unconvincingly)* Oh, how I've longed for a decorating ministry! But it's just not my gifting.

(They all put their phones down.)

ALL: *(Together)* The trouble with the church today is it just doesn't involve young people!

TAKING IT FURTHER

Bible Background: Luke 9:1–6

1. What puts people off helping out in church?
2. What kinds of excuse do the people in the sketch put forward?
3. Read the Bible Background. How do you think the disciples felt about this task? How would the people in the sketch have reacted?

4. Why do you think it's important for people to get involved in church activities?

5. Are there areas in your church that need personnel? Is there any way in which you could help?

16. Just a Little Drink

Topic: Alcohol.

Characters: JOHN.

Setting: This sketch is a fairly demanding piece, requiring the actor to move progressively through ever more drunken stages. JOHN starts sober – at least, apparently so. In between each 'scene' he should turn away from the audience, pause briefly and then turn back. For the bulk of the sketch, JOHN stands at the bar. For the final speech, the location has changed. He might be at home, he might even be in a police cell. This change of locale can be suggested to the audience by having JOHN take off his jacket and tie and sit down on a chair in the middle of the stage. The change of locale will also be suggested by the fact that, in the final speech, JOHN is horribly, brutally sober.

Props/costume: Glass. Chair. Jacket. Tie.

> (JOHN *is standing by the bar. He has a drink in his hand. He is cheerful and friendly.*)

JOHN: Come, on – a little drink never hurt anyone. I mean, it's all about balance, isn't it? It's all about knowing what you can handle. You take me. You see, I can handle it. I can. I mean, I've had, what, four pints tonight so far and I'm perfectly sober. Perfectly sober . . . What was I saying? Oh yeah, four pints. Perfectly sober. Care for another one? *(To Barman)* Same again, mate.

(Turning back to audience) You see some people can't take their alcohol. Some people haven't got the head for it. They're the kind of people who are the problem drinkers. Not me. I've been drinking since I was 16. Not all the time, obviously. I mean, I've taken the odd break. No, but seriously, I don't have a problem handling it at all. Never have.

(He turns away from the audience, briefly. When he turns to face them again he is noticeably more slurred.)

JOHN: No, you take it from me, a little drink never hurt anyone. In fact, just the opposite. The thing is, drinking, it's good for you. No, no, no, all the reports say it. Red wine is good for conories, corroro . . . conrar . . . heart attacks. And if you drink wine, right, you live longer. 'S true. By my reckoning I'm going to make it to 125, judging by the amount I've put away tonight.

And anyway, you've got to enjoy yourself in life, haven't you? That's what life's all about, isn't it? 'S about goin' out on Friday night and havin' a few drinks with the lads. Everyone does it. 'Cos work, an' all that – you want to forget about that. I work hard – 14 hours a day, Monday to Friday. I like to enjoy myself at the weekend. Go down the pub. Go to a party.

I've had some great times at parties. At least, I think I've had some great times at parties. I mean, I can't actually remember anything about them. 'S a funny thing, I always wake up with a traffic cone on my head. Don't matter where I am in the world – I've been drunk all over the globe and every morning it's always the same. Lying in a bush with a traffic cone on my head. *(Fondly)* I met Julie at a party.

(He turns away again. When he faces the audience again he is drunk.)

JOHN: A little drink never hurt no one. No one at all. No sir. No siree. Ignore all those wet blankets. Went to see the doctor and he said I had a drink problem. I said, 'Course I have, mate, have you seen the price of a pint these days?' He rattled on all about liver and kidneys and whatever. Doctors – they make you sick.

(Angry) I mean all you're trying to do is relax, right? Get away from life for a few hours. Get away from Julie. I don't know what's come over that woman. I mean you live with someone, you think you know them and then they change. I keep telling her I can handle it.

(Beckoning towards the audience, as if inviting someone to listen to a confidence) Come here, come here, let me tell you something. I hate my life. Thass why I'm here, innit? *(Louder)* Thass why we're all here. Just want to feel good. Feel great. Get out of my head, get drunk, throw up. Thass what enjoying yourself is all about. Nothing better, eh? Nothing better than a few bevvies. *(Sadly)* I hate my life.

(He turns away again. When he turns back to the audience he has taken off his jacket and his tie, so he is in his shirt sleeves. He is sober. He is in a cell.)

JOHN: It was just a little drink . . . I never meant to hurt anyone. I just . . . Last night when I got in, Julie was there. Usual stuff – row, shouting. I couldn't stand it any more. Got in the car and went for a drive. I suppose I just wanted to get away.

(Pause) I never saw the kid at all.

(Pause) I only had a little drink. I never wanted to hurt anyone.

TAKING IT FURTHER

Bible Background: Proverbs 23:20–21; Ephesians 5:18

1. Why does John drink?
2. What do you think he means by saying 'It's all about balance'?
3. Why do you think John hates his life? How does drinking help him?
4. 'Everyone does it' – Is this a good reason for drinking?
5. 'A little drink never hurt anyone' – Is this true?
6. As Christians, should we drink alcohol at all? How much is OK?

17. Everything Changes

Topic: Change. Nothing lasts for ever.

Characters: CHELSEA; SONIA.

Setting: SONIA's kitchen. There is a table and some chairs on stage. The girls sit and drink from their mugs of coffee while contemplating the futility of existence.

Props/costume: Chairs. Table. Coffee mugs. Empty biscuit barrel.

(*CHELSEA and* SONIA *are sitting at a table, drinking coffee.* CHELSEA *sighs. There is a pause. She sighs again, longer. There is another pause. She then gives a final, huge sigh.*)

SONIA: You're depressed, aren't you?

CHELSEA: I am so bored.

SONIA: Me too.

CHELSEA: You know I'm so bored I even resorted to watching *Trisha*.

SONIA: I didn't realise it was that bad.

CHELSEA: I went to the doctor, and she said it was my mid-life crisis.

SONIA: Oh. (*Pause*) You're only 23.

CHELSEA: That's what I thought. But I was too bored to argue. I mean, remember when you was young?

SONIA: No.

CHELSEA: *(Depressed again)* No, nor me. Memory's going as well. I mean – is this what life's all about? Work and then home, and then sleep, work and then home, and then sleep . . . Sometimes I think there must be something more to life than all this. Then I look at my Trevor snoring in front of the TV, and it starts to rain, and the cat throws up in the aspidistra. I mean, do you ever wonder about things?

SONIA: *(Thinks)* No.

CHELSEA: I do. I was watching this programme last night about the pyramids.

SONIA: Oh, I like them. My mum says the circular teabags are better, but I don't agree –

CHELSEA: *(Interrupting)* The pyramids in Egypt. These rulers built them all those years ago, to secure their place in eternity. One last desperate fight against death and decay.

SONIA: Still, never mind, eh?

CHELSEA: I hate that. I mean, the way things don't last for ever. The way things disappear.

SONIA: Like *Take That*. One minute they have the world at their feet, and the next minute, they've split up.

CHELSEA: Yes, well, it's been quite a few years now, Sonia. I think you should be getting over it.

SONIA: *(Upset)* I wouldn't mind if only Gary could have another hit!

CHELSEA: I was thinking more about things like love and happiness.

SONIA: *(Recovering quickly)* Oh, them.

CHELSEA: How fleeting they all are.

SONIA: Yeah, well, that's life, isn't it? Never mind, eh?

CHELSEA: But doesn't it worry you?

SONIA: There's no point worrying about it, is there? I

mean there's enough to worry about without worrying about things.

CHELSEA: I've been thinking. Everything I like, everything I care about – it will all die eventually. Nothing lasts for ever.

SONIA: *(Pause)* Diamonds.

CHELSEA: Eh?

SONIA: You know – that Shirley Bassey song. 'Diamonds Are Forever'.

CHELSEA: Not if someone nicks them they're not. No, I'm afraid you have been misled, Sonia, by the title of a film and the beguiling charm of Shirley Bassey. Even diamonds, in time, will wear out.

SONIA: True love. That lasts for ever.

CHELSEA: *(Sarcastically)* Hah.

SONIA: Don't you love your Trevor?

CHELSEA: Well, yes. But he won't be around for ever, will he? One day I will walk in to find him slumped in front of the telly, unmoving, unthinking, his eyes a glassy stare.

SONIA: *(Pause)* He's like that now, isn't he?

CHELSEA: Yes, but this time it will be permanent. Even a being as huge and majestic as Trevor will eventually die and decay. Like the dinosaurs. No, let's face it, Sonia, everything is temporary. Love.

SONIA: Happiness.

CHELSEA: Peace.

SONIA: Bus-stops.

CHELSEA: Fulfilment . . . bus-stops?

SONIA: There's a temporary one down the high street because of the roadworks.

CHELSEA: Why can't the good things last for ever? Why does it all have to fade? I'm not asking for much, you know. I'm not asking for life to be a bed of roses. I'm just asking for something permanent. Something so strong that it will never break, and so deep it will never run dry.

SONIA: Oh. *(Pause)* Do you fancy another coffee?

CHELSEA: Yeah, might as well.

SONIA: We've run out of biscuits.

CHELSEA: Oh.

SONIA: Never mind, eh?

CHELSEA: No. Never mind.

TAKING IT FURTHER

Bible Background: John 4:1–30

1. Do you think anything can last for ever?
2. Why do human beings want things to last? Does it bother you?
3. What do you have in your life that is permanent?
4. Read the Bible Background. What kind of life was the woman living? What did Jesus offer her? What difference do you think it made to her life?

18. Care in the Community

Topic: Community.

Characters: DAVID; SIR GERALD.

Setting: A TV studio. DAVID, the interviewer, sits opposite SIR GERALD. Between the two chairs is a small table with the obligatory glasses of water, as in all the best TV interviews.

Props/costume: Two fairly nice-looking chairs. DAVID clutches a clipboard. Small table and two glasses of water. DAVID wears a suit and a fairly modern-looking tie. SIR GERALD is dressed more traditionally, ideally in a pinstripe suit. If you really want to go for laughs, he could always wear a bow-tie. (Well, they make me laugh . . .)

> (DAVID *is an interviewer. He sits opposite* SIR GERALD.)

DAVID: Good evening. I'm here to interview Sir Gerald Fleeby-Greebling, the new Minister for the Community. Good evening, Sir Gerald.

SIR GERALD: Good evening.

DAVID: Now, there has been a lot of talk about your appointment. Can you tell us what the job entails?

SIR GERALD: Well, Robin –

DAVID: No, it's David.

SIR GERALD: Of course, David. Well, it's a very exciting

	challenge. My job is to encourage community feeling and neighbourliness.
DAVID:	Why is community so important?
SIR GERALD:	Well, John –
DAVID:	David.
SIR GERALD:	*(Continuing without a pause)* David, people need to feel like they belong. They need a place they can call home. A place where people care and know about them. A place, Eric, where people know their name.
DAVID:	I see. I understand that some of your work will be encouraging communities to be more welcoming.
SIR GERALD:	Absolutely, Simon.
DAVID:	David.
SIR GERALD:	David. You see community isn't just about what *I want*. It's about what I can do for the people around me. How I can help them. It's about giving as well as getting. A bit like being a cabinet minister, may I say. I mean, yes, there is the government salary and the Bentley and the large expense account. But I also think I am giving something back.
DAVID:	Like what?
SIR GERALD:	Sorry?
DAVID:	What? What are you giving back?
SIR GERALD:	Er . . . I'm giving . . . er . . . I'm giving interviews, for one thing. And Christmas cards. Let my political opponents say what they like, but none of them can accuse me of not giving nice Christmas cards.
DAVID:	I see. Now there has been some comment in the press about your own community.
SIR GERALD:	Oh, Brian, I don't think that we need to

	descend to that level.
DAVID:	Well, with respect, Minister, have you not recently been involved in leading opposition to a new centre for refugees that would have been built near to your village?
SIR GERALD:	That is an entirely different issue, Ahmed. That centre would have made huge inappropriate demands on our area.
DAVID:	But you've just been on about how community is about giving!
SIR GERALD:	Yes, but not to a load of foreigners. Of course we want to give, but only to the right kind of people.
DAVID:	I see. Then there was the time when you opposed a new housing development near your home which was intended to provide low-cost housing for local workers.
SIR GERALD:	Ah, now, Gunter, that site was all wrong. The development would have meant considerable disruption to the home of a notable member of our community.
DAVID:	Who?
SIR GERALD:	Me. I mean, Greebling Hall is a lovely old listed building. All those houses would have led to increased traffic.
DAVID:	I see. What's been built on that site now?
SIR GERALD:	*(Pretending not to know the answer)* Er ... I'm not quite sure ...
DAVID:	Isn't it going to be a car park?
SIR GERALD:	It ... er ... it might be ...
DAVID:	A car park for the tourists who are now visiting 'Greebling-land', the amusement park attached to your stately home?
SIR GERALD:	Yes, well, Jean-Paul –
DAVID:	David.

SIR GERALD: Whatever, you're taking things out of context. That is an important development that employs many local people.

DAVID: Apparently all your workers are bussed in from South Wales because – and I quote – 'labour is cheaper there'.

SIR GERALD: Yes, well, I didn't say they were local to me, did I? They are local to . . . er . . . Cardiff.

DAVID: So what it boils down to, Minister, is that you are all for community values, provided they only apply to someone else's community.

SIR GERALD: No, no, no. It's just that, like all principles, they need to be applied carefully. Community values aren't for everyone's benefit, you know.

DAVID: Thank you, Minister.

SIR GERALD: Thank you, Henry.

DAVID: No, it's David.

SIR GERALD: Of course, Frank.

TAKING IT FURTHER

Bible Background: Leviticus 19:34

1. What do you think we mean by 'community'?
2. 'Of course we want to give, but only to the right kind of people.' Are there any news stories that might illustrate this kind of thinking? Is it necessarily wrong?
3. Why is it important for people to have somewhere they feel they belong?
4. How can churches and Christians help to build communities?
5. Read the Bible Background. What does this tell us about the way we should treat strangers or people new to our community?

19. The Interview

Topic: Persecution.

Characters: PASTOR; OFFICER; GUARD.

Setting: Prison.

Props/costume: Desk. Two chairs. Blindfold. Brown file, including papers and letters. The PASTOR is in his shirt-sleeves. The OFFICER should, if possible, wear a military-style combat jacket and trousers. He does not have to look too official, but military enough to suggest that he is the one in charge. The sketch is based on the true story of a pastor in Somalia, so the dress could reflect that of various African militias that we see all too often on the news.

> *(A cell. At a desk sits the* PASTOR. *He is blindfolded. The* OFFICER *stands behind him.)*

OFFICER: So, you deny the accusation?
PASTOR: I am not aware that any accusation has been made.
OFFICER: You know perfectly well what I am talking about. Your persistent engagement in 'anti-social' activities.
PASTOR: There is nothing anti-social in what I do. People meet together. We talk, we learn, we sing. How can that be anti-social?
OFFICER: It depends what they're singing, doesn't it? When ignorant people gather together to share their

ignorance, then that is anti-social. You know as well as I do that unauthorised meetings are forbidden. Who knows what revolutions you are plotting!

PASTOR: We are not revolutionaries – at least not in the sense that you mean.

OFFICER: You don't deny that charge, then?

PASTOR: I don't deny that our faith changes people. Change enough people and you can change the world. That is what I mean by being a revolutionary. But we have no interest in overthrowing the state. We are not interested in your kind of power. We are simply meeting to worship God together.

OFFICER: Don't speak to me of your God! It is not the true faith.

PASTOR: There I would have to disagree with you.

OFFICER: (Angry) So, you are a blasphemer as well as a revolutionary!

PASTOR: I believe in Jesus Christ. That is all. If that is illegal, then there is no way that I can avoid breaking the law.

OFFICER: You could stop worshipping.

PASTOR: (Flatly) No. I couldn't.

(The OFFICER comes round to stand in front of the PASTOR and then sits down. He opens a brown file and examines a piece of paper.)

OFFICER: I don't understand you. You have been in prison . . . how many times?

PASTOR: I have lost count.

OFFICER: Well, let's just call it 'a lot', shall we? Over 30 years of your life, it says here.

PASTOR: Something like that, yes.

OFFICER: That is a lot of your life to waste. I mean, how does your wife feel? Doesn't she miss you? *(Leaning forward)* Do you know what she gets up to when you are behind bars?

PASTOR: Yes. It worries me very much.

OFFICER: *(Surprised at this admission)* It does?

PASTOR: Yes. I worry about who has to eat her cooking when I am not there.

OFFICER: Very funny.

PASTOR: Anyway, I do not know where she is. The war makes it impossible to find her. I can only trust in God. She will be OK. Her cooking will protect her.

OFFICER: You joke, but you don't fool me. You are scared.

PASTOR: Of course I am. I am only human. I do not want to be locked up. I am frightened that you will beat me again. My only consolation is that God is with me.

OFFICER: You are a fool.

PASTOR: Yes. You will find there are millions of fools, just like me.

OFFICER: I don't think you truly understand your predicament. This will not be like last time, old man. Every time we put you in prison, you talk to others, spreading your insidious beliefs. This time will be different. You will be locked up, forgotten, totally alone.

PASTOR: On the contrary, it is you who don't understand. Put me in prison, I will still be freer than you; lock me up, I will still be at liberty; take away my business, I will still have work to do; separate me from my family and I will be closer to my father than ever. That really scares you, doesn't it? You are scared because you can never truly keep me in prison.

OFFICER: You speak nonsense. This time you will not be released. You will be forgotten.

PASTOR: I think not. People will pray. People all over the world.

OFFICER: You are even more stupid than I thought. Do you really think that they will pray for you, write to you? Yes, some wrote last time. *(Picking letters from the file)* Letters, from New York, from London, from . . . *(Peers)* Milton Keynes – wherever that is. They will forget you. They are too wrapped up in their own world. Their world of televisions and Western goods. Their faith is weak and feeble. They will not pray for you. They will be too busy.

PASTOR: Some, perhaps. Others will remember. We are Christians. We pray for each other.

OFFICER: Well, you will have plenty of opportunity. *(Calls)* Take him away.

(A GUARD enters and leads the PASTOR away. The OFFICER stands and puts on his jacket. He picks up the file, takes out a letter and starts to read.)

TAKING IT FURTHER

Bible Background: Hebrews 13:3

1. Why do you think people are persecuted because of their beliefs?
2. How do you think you would feel if you were treated this way?
3. Read the Bible Background. What obligation does this place on Christians?
4. Think what you can do practically to help victims of injustice and political prisoners.

20. The Purpose of Bernard

Topic: The purpose of life.

Characters: BRAIN; INTESTINE; NERVES.

Setting: The sketch takes place inside Bernard. Actually, it's more like a committee meeting, with the cast sitting in chairs around a table, working through an agenda. On the table is a phone.

Props/costume: A phone. Maybe some notes for the meeting. Table. Three chairs.

(The cast are sitting in a meeting.)

BRAIN:	Right, are we all ready? Good. I now declare the meeting of the Bernard Quigley Management Team open. Is everybody here? Intestines?
INTESTINES:	Here.
BRAIN:	Nervous System?
NERVES:	Here.
BRAIN:	Waste Disposal System?
NERVES:	Sorry – he sends his apologies. He's got a lot on at the moment.
INTESTINES:	Yes. Bernard's mum gave him some curry last night. I've only just finished processing it myself. I mean, fancy giving onion bhaji to a baby! It's just asking for trouble.
BRAIN:	Anyway, the point of this meeting is to decide

97

one simple issue. As his brain, and therefore, if I may so put it, the head of young Bernard, I thought it would be good if we decided on the purpose of the little chap's life.

INTESTINES: Well, I think that's obvious, isn't it? Bernard exists to eat, drink and throw up. That's all he does.

NERVES: He is only seven months old.

INTESTINES: So? He's a bloke. Trust me, loads of blokes go through their entire lives doing exactly the same thing. No – human beings are simply animals.

BRAIN: There must be more to life than that! I mean, I'm his brain. I know I don't have a lot to do at the moment, but in time he will start to talk. Just think of what he'll be able to do!

INTESTINES: Yes! *(Pause)* He'll be able to order a lager and kebab. And say, 'Excuse me please, I think I'm going to be sick.'

NERVES: Look, will you stop going on about that! You only think of his stomach.

INTESTINES: I'm the intestines. What else should I think about?

NERVES: Well, I think about other things. Speaking on behalf of everyone in the nervous system, I think he should immerse himself in sensory pleasures. You know, fine wines, wonderful music, silk sheets . . . the physical sensations.

BRAIN: But all that is so . . . so temporary. I think his purpose is to feed his mind. To increase his knowledge. We should open his mind to literature, to philosophy –

INTESTINES: *(Mocking)* 'We should open his mind to literature!' What a load of rubbish! Open his mouth to grub; that's what he needs.

NERVES: No, no, no, only the body matters. Only what you *feel*.

BRAIN: Oh, this is getting us nowhere! We need to find a single statement, something that the whole body can agree to, something that will give Bernard a purpose to his life. Something that tells him what's really important.

(The phone rings.)

BRAIN: Excuse me. *(He picks up the phone)* Oh. It's you.

INTESTINES: Who is it?

BRAIN: It's Soul. *(Into phone)* Yes, yes, we were discussing that. Yes, I know you deal with the eternal things, but we don't need you at the moment.

INTESTINES: Tell him everyone gets along perfectly well without him.

BRAIN: *(Into phone)* Look, I appreciate that you have a concern, but don't you think that it's just a bit early to be thinking about that sort of thing? He's only a baby. Yes, yes – well, we'll call you if we need you.

(He puts down the phone.)

BRAIN: Honestly – the nerve of some people. *(Looking at NERVES)* No offence.

NERVES: I know what you mean. Just because we're trying to decide what the point of existence is, he starts to stick his nose in.

INTESTINES: We don't need all his rubbish about love and compassion and belief and all that. All we need is to eat, drink and be merry –

NERVES: For tomorrow we –

BRAIN: *(Interrupting)* Yes, well, perhaps we'd better adjourn the meeting there for now. We'll come back to this another time. Say, about 70 years' time.

NERVES: Quite right. There's no need to rush, is there?

INTESTINES: Plenty of time.

BRAIN: I'm sure everything will sort itself out. In the long run.

(They exit. On the table, the phone starts to ring.)

TAKING IT FURTHER

Bible Background: Luke 12:16–23

1. 'Human beings are simply animals.' Do you agree?
2. 'The intestines' talks about eating and drinking; 'Nerves' talks about feelings and sensations; 'Brain' talks about philosophy and thought. What areas do you think 'Soul' would talk about?
3. What kinds of thing give your life purpose?
4. Read the Bible Background. What does this tell us about the purpose of life?

21. Strangers in a Strange Land

Topic: Asylum seekers.

Characters: ONE – a middle-aged, opinionated woman; TWO – her middle-aged but slightly less opinionated friend.

Setting: A coffee bar or tearoom. The impression should be of two women chatting over a cup of tea after a morning's shopping.

Props/costume: Table. Two chairs. Two cups and saucers.

(ONE and TWO sit, sipping tea and watching the world go by.)

ONE: Look, no one could call me an intolerant woman.
TWO: Of course not.
ONE: Live and let live, that's always been my motto.
TWO: Certainly has, certainly has.
ONE: The world would be a better place if we all just showed people a little bit more respect.
TWO: Exactly.
ONE: All I'm saying is, why do these asylum seekers have to come here?
TWO: Are they here, then?
ONE: They are all over the place, my girl. They are flooding across the borders in unprecedented numbers.
TWO: Oh. Why is that, then?
ONE: Just because we have a better standard of living, that's

101

why. It's called 'economic migration'. They are here to take our jobs.

TWO: Oh. *(Pause)* Well, I don't mind.

ONE: What?

TWO: I don't mind if they take mine. I'm fed up with it. Standing out there, facing hordes of dangerous creatures coming at you from all directions, and all the time dealing with huge amounts of toxic waste.

ONE: What do you do, then?

TWO: I'm a dinner lady. They can do that if they want.

ONE: No, you're missing the point. If they take your job, what are you going to do then, eh? How are you going to make a living?

TWO: Oh. I see.

ONE: And it's not even as if their stories are real. Now, you take that couple –

TWO: *(Interrupting)* Pop star.

ONE: *(Surprised)* Sorry?

TWO: I'd like to be a pop star.

ONE: What are you on about?

TWO: Well, if they do my dinner lady job, I could be a pop star.

ONE: No, no, you don't understand –

TWO: Or a supermodel.

ONE: No listen –

TWO: *(Ignoring her)* I could do the walk and everything. I mean, supermodels don't have to dish out mashed potato, do they?

ONE: You're missing the point. You can't just go and be a pop star.

TWO: Why not?

ONE: Well, for one thing you've got a voice that sounds like a hippo with bronchitis. And for another thing, the asylum seekers will have got there first. They'll be the supermodels and the dinner ladies and the pop stars. That's why they've come. To steal our work. Because they're poor and we're rich.

TWO: Well . . . we are quite well off in this country, aren't we?

ONE: We are indeed. And that's the point. We have to keep that. That's our hard-earned wealth. But they come over with their stories of political persecution . . .

TWO: Oh. Poor things.

ONE: No, you see, that's just it. I mean take a look at that couple over there – the couple with the baby. Came across the border this morning. They 'claim' they can't go home. They 'claim' their country's leader will kill the boy. Ridiculous! They're just peasants – anyone can see that.

TWO: But if they haven't got anywhere else to go.

ONE: Oh, don't be daft. There is always somewhere else to go. As long as it's not here. I mean, you'd think we'd learn. We've had huge waves of immigration in the past and look what happened. Frogs, boils, locusts, flies, rivers of blood. It was a nightmare.

TWO: Yes, well, as I recall we did mistreat them.

ONE: That is just namby-pamby liberal propaganda. Those Israelites were born to be slaves. All I'm saying is that we don't want to risk damaging the economic miracle that is first-century Egypt. And as for Herod wanting to kill that baby boy, that's just ridiculous. It's obviously a trumped-up story just to get them their papers.

TWO: Well, I feel sorry for them. Look at her – she's just a kid. And already a refugee.

ONE: You're too soft, you are. If it were down to me, I'd send them all back where they came from. After all, it's not as if they are anyone very important.

TAKING IT FURTHER

Bible Background: Deuteronomy 10:17–22

1. Why do people seek asylum in this country?
2. Do you think that some asylum seekers are bogus?
3. What should be our response to those asking to stay? Should we welcome them all? Or just some? None?
4. Read the Bible Background. What is God saying here?
5. Jesus was a refugee and asylum seeker (see Matthew Chapter 2). Do you think that should alter our opinion of them?

22. Nothing At All

Topic: Standing up against evil.

Characters: ONE; TWO; THREE.

Setting: Plain stage. The actors have to convey the transition from children to teenagers to adults. Rather than attempt this through costume, which would be too time-consuming, it is easier to do it through tone of voice and stance. The children should be hyperactive and fidgety, and talk in that slightly breathless, excitable way that children do. The teenagers should slouch and talk in a more whining, complaining tone of voice (not that I'm stereotyping, you understand . . .). The adults should be much more guarded and defensive. The actual transitions can be marked by the cast simply turning away from the audience and then turning back to face them again.

Props/costume: None.

> (*Enter* ONE, TWO *and* THREE. *They are three children, about primary school age.*)

ONE: It isn't our fault!

TWO: We didn't want to do it.

THREE: I said to him, I said, 'Don't take Sophie's lunch – Miss Henderson will be cross!'

TWO: But he just called me a wimp.

ONE: And he's bigger than we are, see.

TWO: Much bigger.

THREE: And he can do Chinese burns and all that.

ONE: Which really, really, really hurt.

TWO: And we are supposed to be a gang, right?

ONE: So we had to go along with it.

THREE: I didn't even like her sandwiches. I like Marmite.

ONE: So it wasn't really us.

TWO: It was him.

THREE: He made us.

ALL THREE: *(Together)* We didn't do anything at all.

(Pause. They are now teenagers.)

ONE: It isn't our fault!

TWO: We didn't want to do it.

THREE: I said to him, 'Don't set fire to the paper recycling bin. It's dangerous!'

TWO: But he just called me a wimp.

ONE: And he's bigger than we are, see.

TWO: Much bigger.

THREE: And sometimes, even though I'm his friend, I think he might turn on me.

ONE: I've seen him turn on others.

TWO: I mean, we are his mates, at the end of the day.

ONE: So we had to go along with it.

THREE: I spent ages in A&E. But they say the burns will go in time.

ONE: So it wasn't really us.

TWO: It was him.

THREE: He made us.

ALL THREE: *(Together)* We didn't do anything at all.

(Pause. They are adults now.)

ONE: Look, it isn't our fault.

TWO: We didn't want to do it.

THREE: I said to them, 'Look, do you think this is wise? I mean, do we really know these people are guilty?'

TWO: But they just called me a 'collaborator'.

ONE: And there were such a lot of them in the crowd.

TWO: Loads of them.

THREE: And they began to look at me suspiciously.

ONE: Well, I'd seen what they can do.

TWO: And after all, they are our neighbours.

ONE: So we had to go along with it.

THREE: I saw the look on his face as they chased him down the street.

TWO: A group of them caught him. I . . . I don't know what happened next.

THREE: I looked away.

ONE: So it wasn't really us.

TWO: It was them.

THREE: They made us.

(Pause.)

ALL THREE: *(Together)* We didn't do anything at all.

TAKING IT FURTHER

Bible Background: Psalm 1:1–3

1. Why did the three people in this sketch 'go along with it'?
2. Have there been times when you have 'gone along' with something you know is wrong?
3. What could they have done differently? What would have been the consequences?

4. 'It's not my fault.' Do you think they are to blame? If so, why?

5. 'All it takes for evil to triumph is for good people to do nothing.' Can you think of examples where this has been the case?

23. Training School

Topic: Fashion. Appearance. Being 'cool'.

Characters: ASSISTANT – a hyper-trendy, slightly intimidatingly cool shop assistant; KEVIN – not trendy, and not even remotely cool.

Setting: Shoeshop. The ASSISTANT should look at KEVIN as though he is doing him an incredible favour merely by acknowledging KEVIN's existence. KEVIN responds to this not by walking out but by being rather pathetically grateful.

Props/costume: Two pairs of trainers and shoeboxes. Credit card.

(A trendy shoeshop. Enter KEVIN.)

ASSISTANT: Can I help you?

KEVIN: Yes, I'm looking for a pair of training shoes.

ASSISTANT: *(Disdainfully)* 'Training shoes'.

KEVIN: Yes.

ASSISTANT: You haven't bought a pair recently, have you?

KEVIN: Well, no. I'm a bit unfit, you see. Thought I'd do a bit of jogging.

ASSISTANT: Well, we've got a wide range of styles here. How about these? The Adibok 'Air Plus – Pump-Action Super Max', for example. They've got the air-filled sole, neon laces and little lights that flash on and off as you walk along.

KEVIN: I don't want to walk; I want to run.

ASSISTANT: Oh, you can't run in these; they're far too heavy.

KEVIN: Why wear them, then?

ASSISTANT: Well, it's a fashion statement, innit? You go out clubbing; you don't want to look like an antique; you want to look good.

KEVIN: Well, yes –

ASSISTANT: And these are on special offer. Up until 10:45 this morning they were very hip, but they're a bit out of date now.

KEVIN: But it's only 11:30.

ASSISTANT: Things move fast in the fashion world.

KEVIN: Well, they're too heavy for me. What about those?

ASSISTANT: Oh, yes, good choice. The classic two-stripe. Simple, understated, functional –

KEVIN: *(Reading the price tag)* £99.95!

ASSISTANT: – expensive.

KEVIN: £99.95! That's nearly a hundred pounds!

ASSISTANT: *(Sarcastically)* There's no fooling you, is there? Fashion doesn't come cheap. And at least you know these won't go out of date –

KEVIN: Good.

ASSISTANT: – for at least three weeks.

KEVIN: Are they any good for running?

ASSISTANT: Brilliant. Fab. Just don't get them wet.

KEVIN: Sorry?

ASSISTANT: Well, the colour tends to run a bit. I had a mate who went out in a purple pair and it started to rain. It took him three weeks to get the colour off his feet. His feet looked like two bunches of beetroot. He had to tell everyone it was blood pressure.

KEVIN: What's the use of a pair of trainers you can't get wet?

ASSISTANT: Don't you understand? People judge by appearances. It's not who you are; it's what you wear.
You wear these and you will be marked down as
a man of taste, a man who knows his style. You
will be a fashion-god!

(KEVIN is mesmerised. He hands over his credit card.)

KEVIN: I'll take them.
ASSISTANT: I knew you'd see sense. Everyone does, in the end.

TAKING IT FURTHER

Bible Background: James 2:1–4

1. Do you think fashion is important?
2. How much would you spend on a pair of trainers? Why?
3. 'You go out clubbing . . . you want to look good.' How do you decide what 'looks good'?
4. 'It's not who you are; it's what you wear.' Do you agree with this? Do you think it matters what we look like?

24. Video Nasties

Topic: Films. Media influence.

Characters: KEVIN; TINA.

Setting: A living-room. KEVIN and TINA sit on a sofa.

Props/costume: Sofa. DVD box.

(Enter KEVIN, holding a DVD box.)

KEVIN: At last! I've got it!

TINA: What?

KEVIN: *Friday the Thirteenth Part Sixty-Two: The Revenge of the Pencil Sharpener!*

TINA: Yuck.

KEVIN: 'Yuck'? What do you mean, 'yuck'?

TINA: Well, it doesn't sound a very nice film to me.

KEVIN: Oh, what do you know? This is class, this is. *(Reading the label)* 'From the people who brought you *I Know What You Did Last Easter* and *The Texas Cheese Grater Massacre*, a fantastic festival of blood, gore and nauseous special effects.' Doesn't that sound great?

TINA: No. It sounds horrible.

KEVIN: Oh, I suppose you'd prefer we watched one of your costume drama films? What was that last one – *Stench and Stenchability*?

TINA: *Sense and Sensibility*.

113

KEVIN: Same thing. Load of tat. Just a load of posh people sitting around and drinking tea. Not a gun in sight. No one even got knifed.

TINA: Just because no one got killed doesn't make it a bad film.

KEVIN: It does in my book. That's what you want out of a movie – a bit of senseless violence. I mean if one of those posh blokes had suddenly pulled out a machete and gone berserk it might have livened up the film a bit.

TINA: It's based on a Jane Austen novel. She didn't go in for mindless violence.

KEVIN: Well, she should have. She'd have made a lot more money.

TINA: I really don't know what you see in this stuff.

KEVIN: You agreed to watch the last one.

TINA: You tricked me. You told me it was about politics.

KEVIN: Well it was, sort of.

TINA: *The Blair Witch Project* was not about New Labour's religious policy, Kevin, and you know it. You lied to me. Just like you did when you told me that *The Silence of the Lambs* was about organic farming.

KEVIN: You know your trouble? You won't face up to reality. You live in a fantasy world where everyone wears long skirts and lacy bonnets and tight breeches. But life isn't like that, Tina. It's nasty and violent and brutal. It's a cruel, savage jungle out there.

TINA: We live in Sidcup, Kevin. Sidcup is not a savage jungle. At least, Acacia Avenue isn't, anyway.

KEVIN: Well, I'm going to watch my film.

TINA: But haven't you ever wondered what all this endless diet of violence is doing to us?

KEVIN: Oh, don't bring that up! We've had this conversation before. Movies reflect society; they don't shape it.

TINA: If that's so, why do they bother to advertise?

KEVIN: Eh?

TINA: Look at every movie. They've all got product place-
        ment, haven't they? James Bond drives a certain kind
        of car, drinks a certain kind of drink. The manufac-
        turers pay to have him do that, because they know
        that people will copy him.

KEVIN: That's an entirely different thing.

TINA: It's not. You can't argue that films have no effect
        when people copy them all the time. I mean look at
        The Matrix. For three weeks after you saw that film,
        you wandered around dressed in black and kept
        bending over backwards to avoid the imaginary
        bullets. It was like living with a very depressed limbo
        dancer.

KEVIN: Yes, but just because you copy some things in a
        movie, it doesn't mean you're going to copy every-
        thing. I mean you've sat through some of my favour-
        ite movies and you've never been tempted to go out
        and shoot anyone, have you?

TINA: *(Pause)* Only the writer and director. And the idiot
        who paid three quid to the video shop to rent it in the
        first place.

KEVIN: Well, I don't care. I like a bit of violence. You just
        want to spoil my fun.

TINA: I don't. I just think you should think about what you
        watch.

KEVIN: And so should you. All those films about posh
        people in big frocks – I mean, are they any better? All
        that rosy-eyed view of the past. And all those films
        where one beautiful person meets another beautiful
        person and, after a series of hilarious misunder-
        standings, they eventually get together. Nobody is
        ever ugly in those films, are they? Nobody ever has a

dull job or lives in a small, poky house, or sweats or breaks wind. If my shoot-'em-ups influence society, so do your costume dramas.

TINA: You're right. Maybe we should both ask more questions.

KEVIN: Good. Now, I'm going to fetch a beer and watch this masterpiece of the horror genre.

TINA: I don't think you are, actually.

KEVIN: Oh, right. Censorship, is it? You are curtailing my right to view.

TINA: Well, it's up to you. But I do think that you are going to find difficulty putting this into our video player.

KEVIN: Why?

TINA: It's a DVD, you idiot!

TAKING IT FURTHER

Bible Background: Philippians 4:8

1. What kinds of film do you like? What kinds of world do they show?
2. Do you think that films influence society? Has a film ever influenced you?
3 Kevin argues that people copy some things and not others. Do you agree?
4. 'I just think you should think about what you watch.' How could we do this?
5. 'Maybe we should both ask more questions.' What kinds of question would help us to understand a film's influence?

25. Dream on . . .

Topic: Hopes and ambitions.

Characters: SCOTT; SANDRA; JULIE.

Setting: A school classroom. SCOTT, SANDRA and JULIE sit at a table with their school books open in front of them.

Props/costume: Leaflet. Table. Three chairs. School books. If possible, all the cast should wear school uniform.

> (SCOTT, SANDRA and JULIE are sitting at the back during a lesson in school.)

SCOTT: What are you going to do when all this is finished?

SANDRA: I'm going to go home and have my tea.

SCOTT: No, no, I don't just mean this lesson. I mean the whole thing. School. Education and all that.

SANDRA : Oh. I'm going to college. Get qualified.

JULIE : Yeah? What are you going to do at college, then?

SANDRA: I'm either going to do Advanced Philosophy and Situational Ethics, or Plumbing. I haven't decided yet.

JULIE: You could combine them both. It would be great – you know, 'Install your washing machine, madam? And while we're at it, have you thought about the meaning of life?'

SANDRA: Yeah. Good idea. I could be the world's first philosopher-plumber. I can see it now: 'Sandra

117

	Podule – Plumber and General Thinker.' That'd look great on the side of a van, that would.
SCOTT:	What about you?
JULIE:	Oh, I'm going to university. Going to study Pharmacy.
SCOTT:	Pharmacy. Yeah, I can just see you behind the counter in Boots, handing out the paracetamol.
JULIE:	There's more to it than that. I'm going to work overseas.
SANDRA:	Do Boots have many branches overseas, then?
JULIE:	In hospitals or clinics. *(She pulls a leaflet from her pocket)* Look, this is the kind of thing. Working with aid agencies in refugee camps or in slum areas.
SANDRA:	*(Examining the crumpled leaflet)* You carry this around with you?
JULIE:	Yeah. Well, it's kind of a dream of mine.
SCOTT:	There's no money in it, is there? Not exactly the grandest of dreams.
SANDRA:	Well, what about you, then?
SCOTT:	Isn't it obvious?
JULIE:	I don't know. Village idiot?
SCOTT:	Nah – I'm going to be a male supermodel.

(There is a silence.)

SANDRA:	How do you work that out, then?
SCOTT:	Well, I've got everything you need. I'm young, I'm virile, with a winning smile. *(He smiles, unconvincingly)*
JULIE:	Yes. Now, I hate to be the one to break this to you, Scott, but you do need other attributes.
SCOTT:	What do you mean?
JULIE:	Well, how can I put this kindly? You're not exactly conventionally handsome, are you?

SCOTT: You don't know nothing, you don't. I'm quirkily
           attractive. And I've got smouldering good looks.

           (He smoulders.)

SANDRA: Are you all right?
SCOTT: I'm smouldering.
SANDRA: Oh. I thought you had the cramp.
SCOTT: And with my dress sense, I could start doing mod-
           elling for catalogues.
JULIE: I didn't know the Salvation Army clothes banks
           issued a catalogue.
SCOTT: You can mock –
JULIE: Thank you.
SCOTT: – but we all have our dreams.
JULIE: Yes, but that's not enough, is it? There's a difference
           between dreams and complete fantasies.
SCOTT: What are you saying?
JULIE: Oh, get real, Scott. Nothing personal, but you are
           not going to get a sudden call from Calvin Klein
           asking you to hop up onto the catwalk.
SCOTT: It could happen. All right, maybe I'll get a little
           plastic surgery.
JULIE: Scott, you will need more than a little plastic
           surgery. You will need a complete head transplant.
SCOTT: Well at least my dream is a proper dream – you
           know, riches and glamour and all that. That's what
           most people dream about. Pharmacy! People don't
           dream about that! They dream about glamour!
SANDRA: Excitement!
SCOTT: Wealth.
SANDRA: The Turbo 3000 central heating system with the
           balanced flue.

(SCOTT and JULIE look at SANDRA.)

SANDRA: It's a plumbing thing.

JULIE: Maybe, but I'm working towards my dream. I'm going to make mine happen, that's the difference. I mean, what will you do if you don't achieve super-model status?

SCOTT: Eh?

JULIE: What will happen if Calvin never phones?

SCOTT: *(Gloomily)* I dunno. I'll find something.

JULIE: You ought to think about it. It's a terrible thing not to have a dream, not to have something to aim at.

SANDRA: Yeah, who wants to drift through life?

SCOTT: *(Brightening up)* You're right. *(Sneeringly)* Supermodel! What a stupid idea! Nah, I should be more realistic.

JULIE: Glad you've come to your senses.

SCOTT: Yeah. Now, International Super-Spy – that's what I call a job!

TAKING IT FURTHER

Bible Background: Philippians 3:10–14

1. 'Riches and glamour and all that. That's what most people dream about.' Is that true?
2. Do you have dreams and ambitions? What are they?
3. Is there anything you can do to achieve those dreams? Have you thought about what steps you could take?
4. Read the Bible Background. What was Paul's goal? Do your dreams run in the same direction?

26. Making Your Mark

Topic: Voting.

Characters: DARREN; JIM.

Setting: A park bench. DARREN and JIM are just sitting, sipping from two cans of drink. They are obviously at a loose end. JIM is drinking with difficulty because his tooth is hurting. Occasionally he winces in pain.

Props/costume: A bench. Two cans of drink.

> *(DARREN and JIM are sitting on a bench. They are obviously two bored young people. They take swigs from their drinks.)*

DARREN: How's your tooth, then?
JIM: It's fine. Fine. Doesn't hurt at all.
DARREN: Oh.

> *(DARREN pauses for a moment and then pokes JIM in the side of the face.)*

JIM: *(Spitting out his drink)* Owwwwwwwww! What did you do that for?
DARREN: I thought you said your tooth was better.
JIM: It will get better. I don't have to do anything about it. It will cure itself.
DARREN: You ought to go to the dentist.

121

JIM: There's no need. Look, it's fine now, see? No problem.

(DARREN pauses for a moment and then pokes JIM in the side of the face again.)

JIM: Owwwwwwwwww! Will you stop doing that?

DARREN: I'm just proving a point.

JIM: Well, stop it! Leave me alone.

(There is a pause.)

DARREN: So, have you decided who you're going to vote for yet?

JIM: What?

DARREN: This wossname. Generous election. Who are you going to vote for?

JIM: Darren, are you extra-thick or what? I'm not going to vote.

DARREN: Why not?

JIM: Oh, look around you, Darren! Look at the world. Open your eyes. Do you think that any of the people in power care about us? Do you think that they're interested in us?

DARREN: They might be. They have different wossnames. Polyfillas.

JIM: Policies.

DARREN: Them as well. Like the last lot, they brought in the wossname. The miniskirt wage.

JIM: Minimum wage.

DARREN: That made a difference to me. Before that I used to get paid 13 pence and a bag of chips per hour. And I'm sure the other lot have got some good things about them as well.

JIM: You don't understand, do you, Darren? Voting isn't cool.

DARREN: My dad says it's our duty. He says that in some countries people die for the right to vote and that we should take it seriously.

JIM: Oh, and how seriously do those politicians take it? They bombard us with stupid adverts and sound-bytes and treat us like imbeciles. I'm not playing their games.

DARREN: That may be true, but don't you think we ought to at least decide for ourselves?

JIM: Look, Darren, what does it matter? They're all the same, these parties.

DARREN: You know that, do you?

JIM: What?

DARREN: You've read their wossnames, their manifestations. You know what they all stand for?

JIM: Well, of course I haven't waded through all that lot. But I know they're all the same. They're all out for number one.

DARREN: But if that's the case we ought to do something about it.

JIM: Aha! Well, you see that's exactly what I am doing. I am revolting. I am rebelling against the system.

DARREN: Oh. And how are you doing that then?

JIM: What?

DARREN: Well, how exactly are you rebating against the system? I mean, I've never seen you do anything. All you do is sit there scratching yourself and fantasising about getting off with Janice Protheroe. Hardly the act of a great revolutionary, is it? I can't see how that is going to change the political system.

JIM: I am rebelling against the system, Darren, in one simple way. I am refusing to vote.

DARREN: I see. Let me get this right. You are proposing to change the political system by doing absolutely nothing to change the system.

JIM: Exactly.

DARREN: But surely if we all refused to vote, then nothing would change at all.

JIM: No. The system will break down. It will collapse of its own accord, Darren, and a new age of freedom will take its place where all men are brothers and free love abounds. Especially between me and Janice Protheroe. It will happen, Darren. Provided we all get together and do nothing.

(There is a pause. DARREN *pokes* JIM *in the face.)*

JIM: Owwwwwwww!

DARREN: Just proving a point.

TAKING IT FURTHER

Bible Background: Romans 13:1–7

1. Why doesn't Jim want to vote?
2. 'They're all the same, these parties.' Do you agree?
3. Do you think that voting changes anything?
4. 'My dad says it's our duty.' Why do you think he says this?
5. 'They bombard us with stupid adverts.' How can we find out what the parties really stand for? Can we talk to them direct?
6. Is it ever right not to vote?

27. Your Flexible Friend

Topic: Debt.

Characters: ONE; TWO.

Setting: A living-room or similar. TWO sits in a comfy chair reading the paper.

Props/costume: Newspaper. Wallet. Three credit cards. Armchair. Catalogue. Jacket with inside pocket for ONE.

> (TWO *is sitting reading the paper. Enter* ONE, *very excited.*)

ONE: Here, look, it's arrived!

TWO: What is it?

ONE: The solution to all my problems. The key to a new life filled with wealth and riches! A doorway into a world of wonderful clothes and beautiful furniture and little expensive gadgets that you use once and then put in a drawer and forget. And it's all mine!

TWO: *(Pause)* OK. It's one of two things. You've either won the lottery. Or you've been drinking the metal polish again.

ONE: Nope. It's my new credit card.

TWO: A credit card.

ONE: Not just a credit card. If I spend on this I get *(impressively)* extra points!

TWO: For what?

ONE: Eh?

TWO: Points for what?

ONE: Points for . . . er . . . well, if you get lots of points you can trade them in for more things. *(Gets out catalogue)* Look – they've sent me this catalogue. I could get a personal stereo! Or a handy nasal-hair remover. All I have to do is get 100 points.

TWO: And how do you get points?

ONE: Every time you spend £10 you get a point.

TWO: So, let me get this right, to get 100 points you'd have to spend £1,000.

ONE: Er . . . probably.

TWO: Great, so you could be £1,000 in debt and have your own nasal-hair remover!

ONE: It's great, isn't it?

TWO: Fabulous.

ONE: Of course, I'm not going to use this in a stupid and frivolous way. I'm only going to use this card for important items of expenditure.

TWO: Such as?

ONE: *(Producing another card)* Paying off this one.

TWO: Right. *(Thinking about it)* Hang on, you're going to use that card *(pointing at the first card)* to pay off that card *(pointing at second card)*?

ONE: Yes. Clever, huh?

TWO: *(Pointing at second card)* And what did you use that card for?

ONE: Paying off my overdraft.

TWO: They've really got you, haven't they?

ONE: I'll be all right. I'm just paying off some debts from Christmas.

TWO: Christmas.

ONE: And Easter. And Epiphany. And the fourth Thursday in Lent.

TWO: Yes, well, 'lent' is the operative word, really, isn't it?

ONE: And then there was my holiday, the car and all the new stuff for my flat. But I really needed that inflatable sofabed with the built-in aromatherapy unit.

TWO: How much do you owe, then?

(ONE whispers to TWO.)

TWO: *(Shocked)* How much?

ONE: Well, it's all the clothes and stuff, isn't it? I mean, a man in my line of work, he's got to have all the right gear.

TWO: What do you mean, 'your line of work'? You're a dustman.

ONE: Exactly. That's why you've got to have great clobber. You can't pull the girls dressed in an old boiler suit and some Doc Martens, can you?

TWO: But all this borrowing! It must be costing you a fortune.

ONE: No, no, because the interest rate is low. Only about 8% or something.

TWO: Per month.

ONE: What?

TWO: Eight per cent per month. All credit cards are worked out per month. It's more expensive per year. Look – there, it says 18% APR. That means if you have £1,000 on your balance over a year you will pay £180 just in interest.

ONE: Yeah, but it's *credit*, isn't it? You've got to have it. Otherwise you'd have to save up and all that boring kind of stuff. And you can't hire a car or pay for tickets over the phone or any of that stuff unless you've got a credit card.

TWO: But you've got to pay in the end, haven't you?

ONE: Oh, I suppose, eventually. But I can keep this going for years.

TWO: You don't understand what debt is like. It's a chain. You don't get more free by borrowing more. You don't get more liberated by owning more. You just dig deeper into the hole. And it can cripple everything. Did you know that one of the commonest causes of relationship breakdown is worries over money and debt?

ONE: If that's the case, Mr. Smarty-pants-financial-pages-relationship-expert, how come everyone keeps using them?

TWO: Because it's easy. Because it feels like you haven't spent anything. Look, I'm not against it, I'm just saying, be aware of what's going on. Keep tabs. Nothing is easier than getting into debt. And nothing is harder than getting out of it.

ONE: Well, maybe you're right. Maybe I should take some steps. You know, sort out my finances.

TWO: Right.

ONE: And I know just how to do it.

TWO: How?

(ONE says nothing, but smiles. From his inside pocket he pulls out another credit card and holds it up triumphantly.)

TAKING IT FURTHER

Bible Background: Proverbs 10:4; Matthew 6:19–21

1. Is it wrong to own a credit card? What kinds of thing might you need a card for?
2. Have you ever been in debt, or are you in debt at the moment? Do you ever worry about it?

3. 'One of the commonest causes of relationship breakdown is worries over money and debt.' Why might this
   be?
4. How can we stop ourselves running up large debts?
5. Why do so many banks and businesses want us to use
   credit cards?

28. A Lot of Work for Charity

Topic: Why give to charity? Uniqueness of humanity.

Characters: ONE; TWO.

Setting: A railway station. ONE and TWO stand either side of the stage, shaking their collecting tins or buckets.

Props/costume: Collecting tins or buckets. Coins to make a rattling sound.

> (ONE *and* TWO *are collecting for charity. They stand shaking their collecting buckets.*)

ONE: *(Calling to the passers-by)* Help the children!

TWO: Help the homeless children!

ONE: Help the poor homeless children!

TWO: Help the poor homeless children without any legs!

ONE: Help the poor legless homeless children who also have really bad skin conditions and invasive dandruff!

TWO: *(Calling, then stopping)* Help the . . . Oh, I can't be bothered. *(To* ONE*)* How are you doing?

ONE: OK. *(Looking into his collecting bucket)* There's quite a lot of pound coins in there. Not to mention several pesetas, a coat button and a slightly sucked polo mint. How about you?

TWO: *(Depressed)* Oh, fine. Fine.

ONE: Are you all right?

TWO: I think I'm having a bit of a philosophical crisis.

131

ONE: Oh. Do you want a plaster on it?

TWO: I mean, haven't you ever wondered why we do all this?

ONE: What?

TWO: Standing here. Rattling our buckets.

ONE: It's obvious – so that people can give us their money. And their polo mints.

TWO: Yes, but why?

ONE: If we didn't do it things would get worse and worse for them. They'd get poorer and poorer and spottier and spottier and . . . er . . . lose even more legs. So we have to do it.

TWO: Look, every year I stand here on this railway station shaking my bucket. And every year people give their money. Well, apart from the ones who put in the pesetas and the polo mints. Now why do they do that? They're never going to see these people. They're never going to meet them. They live thousands of miles away in their small, crowded, dandruff-ridden slums. So why should the commuters on the 7:19 from Milton Keynes care?

ONE: Well, it's natural for us to feel sorry for those who are worse off than we are.

TWO: No, it can't be natural.

ONE: Why not?

TWO: Well, don't you remember our biology lessons at school? They kept on about how human beings are basically lumps of chemicals and all that. So if that's the case, why do we care? I mean why should I care about another lump of chemicals? Even if they are a poor, legless, homeless, dandruff-ridden lump of chemicals.

ONE: Yes. I see your point. And what was that other thing they used to go on about in biology? That fundamental force of nature –

TWO: Dorothy Prenderghast?

ONE: Who?

TWO: You remember. Big girl. Had a left hook that could fell a horse. She was a force of nature.

ONE: No, no, not her. Wossname. Evolution. 'Law of the jungle' and all that.

TWO: Oh, right. *(Pause)* Still sounds like Dorothy Prenderghast to me.

ONE: No, you know, it's the survival of the fittest. The weakest just die out, leaving only the fittest and strongest to survive.

TWO: *(Suddenly getting the point)* Exactly! And who's to say that isn't what's happening here? Maybe these poor homeless, legless, etc, etc, children are the rejects, and we shouldn't try to preserve them. They are only weakening the gene pool. We should let them go. 'You are the weakest link. Goodbye.'

(They ponder this for a moment, suddenly sad at this thought.)

ONE: I don't believe that.

TWO: No. Neither do I.

ONE: There is something special about people. We are more than just a collection of chemicals. We're more than just some jungle animals fighting it out for survival. We're all special, unique beings.

TWO: Even Dorothy Prenderghast.

ONE: Especially Dorothy Prenderghast. Maybe the point is we care because, deep down, we know that. We know that people are unique. Special.

TWO: But what is it that makes us special?

ONE: I don't know. All I know is that people matter. They are worth caring for. We can't just let them drift away into the darkness.

TWO: Yes. You're right. That must be it. That's why we do this.

ONE: For the special people. Everywhere.

TWO: *(Suddenly shaking his bucket with energy)* Help the children!

ONE: Help the homeless children!

ONE: Help the poor, homeless, very, very special children!

ONE: Help the poor homeless, totally unique children!

TAKING IT FURTHER

Bible Background: Psalm 139:13–16

1. Have you ever raised money for charity? If so, what was it, and why did you do it?
2. 'They are only weakening the gene pool.' Can you think of anyone who has held this view? How did it affect their view of humanity?
3. Why do you think we care about the fate of people thousands of miles away?
4. Do you think that human beings are 'special'? Why? What is it that makes us more than a bundle of chemicals?
5. If human beings are unique, then how should that affect our view of those who are suffering?

29. That's Nice, Dear . . .

Topic: Hypocrisy and duplicity.

Characters: CECILY; BRIAN.

Setting: A living-room or similar. CECILY is reading her newspaper when BRIAN enters. He is back from the office.

Props/costume: Two chairs. Newspaper for CECILY. BRIAN wears a suit, although, as it is the end of the day, he has loosened his tie.

(CECILY *sits reading. Enter* BRIAN.)

CECILY: Hello dear, had a good day?

BRIAN: Fantastic.

CECILY: How did the meeting go?

BRIAN: Well, Monica didn't get the chairmanship. Naturally I was very sympathetic. Gave her all the support I could. Told her what a huge mistake they were making.

CECILY: That's nice, dear.

BRIAN: Well, it would have been except I didn't actually vote for her in the first place.

CECILY: But I thought you told her –

BRIAN: Of course I told her I would vote for her. But it's a secret ballot. I let her think she was getting my secret vote, when all the time I was keeping my secret vote really secret. So she thought she knew

135

my secret, but she didn't know my secret secret. I kept that secret.

CECILY: Oh. That's nice, dear.

BRIAN: And the beauty of it is she still thinks I voted for her. Whereas in fact I voted for Gerald. I said to him, 'Gerald, you're the man for the job. Only you can run this business.'

CECILY: That's nice, dear.

BRIAN: Of course I was lying. Run the business? That man couldn't run a bath. No, the truth is that he'll be absolute putty in our hands. He'll get bogged down in all the paperwork while we make the decisions. I mean we'll let him make *some* decisions, just to make him think he's decisive. But those decisions won't be the decisive decisions.

CECILY: Oh. Won't they?

BRIAN: Of course not. Trevor and I will decide the decisive decisions. That's decided.

CECILY: Oh. That's nice, dear.

BRIAN: And then I saw old Bill at the end of the day. He's ever so anxious. Heard all these noises from central office that we were going to axe his unit. Well, of course, I made all the reassuring noises. Told him that every-thing was under control. You know, calmed him down.

CECILY: Oh. That's nice, dear.

BRIAN: Well, it would be, except he's being sacked next week. Everyone knows it – except him.

CECILY: Don't you think someone ought to tell him?

BRIAN: Don't be silly. If I told him, then he'd know that I know. And if he knows I know, then he'd know that I'd said I didn't know when I knew.

CECILY: I see.

BRIAN: No, best to keep out of it. Pretend ignorance, that's my method. That way no one blames me and everyone thinks I'm on their side. Anyone who is sensible acts this way.

CECILY: That's nice, dear.

BRIAN: Any phone messages?

CECILY: Dorothy phoned. She wanted you to call her back.

BRIAN: Oh no, not that awful woman again! Why should I speak to her?

CECILY: Well, she is your sister.

BRIAN: I can't help that.

CECILY: I thought you told her to call you if she needed you?

BRIAN: I know I said that. Of course I said that. But I didn't mean it. I mean, think of the problems she's got! I didn't think she'd actually take me up on it, for heaven's sake. I'm a busy man.

CECILY: Well, if you said something –

BRIAN: Oh, I know, don't worry. I'll give her a call.

CECILY: That's nice, dear.

BRIAN: Well, it would be, if I was actually listening. Still, let her rabbit on. It seems to do her good. Well, I can't sit here all day. I'd better get on with my preparation.

CECILY: What are you preparing? Another take-over bid? A new proposal?

BRIAN: Of course not. Have you forgotten? I'm leading house group this week. Matthew 5:37 – 'Let your yes be yes and your no be no.'

CECILY: *(Pause)* Oh. That's nice, dear.

TAKING IT FURTHER

Bible Background: Matthew 7:15–23

1. Why does Brian act the way he does in the sketch?
2. The word 'hypocrite' comes from the Ancient Greek word for 'actor'. Why do you think that is?

3. 'Anyone who is sensible acts this way.' Do you agree? If not, why not?

4. Are there times when you have said one thing and meant another?

5. Read the Bible Background. What does Jesus mean by 'good fruit'? What do you think he would say to Brian in the sketch?

30. The Good Book

Topic: The Bible.

Characters: ONE; TWO; THREE; FOUR.

Setting: Bare stage. The cast should speak as if they are talking to someone directly in front of them, as though responding to their questions. It is as if someone is speaking to them, but the audience should be hearing just one side of the conversation. If you find this too difficult, you could give each character a mobile phone to speak into, but I think the sketch has more impact if the characters speak directly to the audience. Try it. You might be pleasantly surprised . . .

Props/costume: Four different-looking Bibles.

> (ONE, TWO, THREE *and* FOUR *stand facing the audience. They are holding Bibles of varying kinds.*)

ONE: Oh, yes, the Bible. What a wonderful book. Do you know how long it took to write it? One thousand, five hundred years. Imagine: a book written over at least 1,500 years! So, if you want to write a new Bible I should start now. It'll be finished some time around 3,500 AD.

TWO: Oh, the Bible! Wonderful. I love the Bible. All those stories. David and Goliath. Noah's ark. Jack and the Beanstalk. I love all those – Sorry? Oh. OK, not Jack

139

and the Beanstalk. But the other ones are in there, aren't they? Lovely.

THREE: What I like about the Bible is that you can use it to find answers. You see, all you have to do is open it up and whatever question you're thinking of, you'll find the answer in there. What? Well, no, no, it doesn't have things like people's telephone numbers. Don't be silly. They didn't use telephones in those days.

FOUR: The thing about the Bible is that it tells us all what we're doing wrong. The Bible is a book of rules. Loads of rules and commands. That's what it's there for. It's the Law.

ONE: And do you know another thing about the Bible? It's not just one book. It's got loads of books in it, all written by different people. That's right. Sixty-six books. More like a library, in fact.

TWO: What's that other story? Um . . . the Prodigal Samaritan. Oh yes, I love that one. It's all about this Samaritan – I think it's someone who works on a telephone helpline or something – anyway, he decides he's going to run away from the Samaritans, and so he goes and takes the money he's owed. But he's beaten up and all his money is stolen by pigs! Or something like that. It's amazing, anyway.

THREE: But the Bible is a book of answers. What? No, it doesn't have a recipe in it for apple crumble. No, no, you're missing the point. It's not the specific questions; it's the general principles. That's what the answers are – Eh? No, well, I'm not sure what the principles are about apple crumble. But they're in the Bible somewhere.

FOUR: I often bless people by telling them how the Bible condemns what they're doing. You see the Bible is all about judgement and condemnation. It shows how many people are sinners. That's why most Bibles are covered in black. It's because we're all doomed.

ONE: *(Impressively)* Over three-quarters of a million words. Just think of that. Centuries of wisdom, hundreds of thousands of words of insight. Pure history.

TWO: And then there's the story of Jesus and all that he did. That's a lovely story as well, because he went about healing people and helping blind people to see and helping lepers . . . er . . . leap. Anyway, he did some lovely things and said some lovely words and it was all lovely. What? They did what to him? Oh, no, no, I'm sure that's not in the Bible. That sounds far too nasty.

THREE: *(Mysteriously)* You see the Bible has so much power. Like when I want the answer to something, I just close my eyes and open it and point my finger and I get the answer. The other day I was offered some work as a builder and I didn't know whether to do it, so I opened the Bible and pointed, and I found Proverbs 26:27 – 'If a man digs a pit, he will fall into it.' So I stayed in bed. Admittedly, I had to open it up and point five times before I came up with the right answer, but I got there in the end.

FOUR: Most of mankind is doomed, you see. Doomed. The Bible tells us that we should weep and wail. Jesus didn't come to spend his time at parties, you know. What? Did he? Well, he probably went to tell them all they were doomed.

ONE: It's a unique historical document. A remarkable account of ancient times and beliefs.

TWO: I've always loved the stories. I used to have them all told to me at Sunday school – that's how I know all about them. I can remember them. It's lovely.

THREE: See, the Bible is a mystery. It's like an oracle or a spirit guide.

FOUR: The Bible is a rulebook. It's God's set of commands to stop us all from being doomed.

ONE: It's a remarkable book. Sorry? Do I what?

TWO: Do I read it?

THREE: What, you mean, not just 'point' at bits?

FOUR: I don't need to read it to know we're all doomed.

ONE: Of course I don't read it. It's full of ancient history.

TWO: Of course I don't read it. I just think about the stories.

THREE: Of course I don't read it. I just dip in to find the answers I want. *(Suddenly correcting himself)* Need.

FOUR: Of course I don't read it. I know how God feels already.

TAKING IT FURTHER

Bible Background: 2 Timothy 3:14–17

1. What do you think about the Bible?
2. How do each of these people view it?
3. Is the Bible full of stories? Or full of rules? Or is it full of history?
4. Can the Bible be of any use today? If so, how?
5. Do you ever read the Bible?

31. I Swear it's a Great Play

Topic: Swearing.

Characters: DIRECTOR; SUSAN.

Setting: A rehearsal studio. The DIRECTOR sits on a chair to the side of the stage. SUSAN stands in the centre of the stage.

Props/costume: Two chairs. Two play scripts.

(The DIRECTOR *is talking to* SUSAN *– an actress – about her role in a new play.)*

DIRECTOR: Right, now, I thought before we started that it would be good for us to talk about your character in the play. You know, get a bit of background.

SUSAN: Great.

DIRECTOR: OK. The character that you play – Angie – is a girl from the wrong side of the tracks.

SUSAN: I see.

DIRECTOR: She's seen the rough side of life. She's not afraid to speak her mind. She's a tough, opinionated woman. She's had to learn how to survive.

SUSAN: Good, good.

DIRECTOR: So, look, here's a piece of dialogue. Maybe you'd like to read it for me.

SUSAN: OK. *(Reads as* ANGIE*)* 'You won't get away with this! You think you can come in and take over this town, but you haven't reckoned with me, you slimy –' *(Realising and coming out of character)* Oh. I'm sorry, I can't say that.

DIRECTOR: *(Taking a look)* Oh, it's pronounced 'you slimy –'

SUSAN: *(Hurriedly interrupting him)* I know how it's pronounced. I just mean that I don't want to say it.

DIRECTOR: Oh. Why not?

SUSAN: Well, it's not very nice, is it? Calling someone that word.

DIRECTOR: But you're playing a hard-bitten character. From the wrong side of the tracks.

SUSAN: Yes, I know that, but I still don't want to say it.

DIRECTOR: All right, all right. We'll talk about it later. Just carry on reading.

SUSAN: Where were we? Oh, yes. *(As* ANGIE *again)* 'You haven't reckoned with me, you slimy – ahem – "person". I'm going to take you apart. I'm going to rip your –' *(Coming out of character again)* Oh. *(She reads a bit further)* Well, that's not a very nice thing to do at all! And I can't say any of these words.

DIRECTOR: What do you mean, 'you can't say them'?

SUSAN: I don't use swear-words. So I can't say them.

DIRECTOR: But it's not *you* saying them. It's Angie.

SUSAN: I don't care. My mum might come and see this play. What's she going to think if she sees me up there using words like this?

DIRECTOR: All right, all right. Leave it for now. Just edit out the ones you don't like and we'll try to find a way round the problem.

SUSAN: OK. I'll bleep them out.

(During the next speech, SUSAN *replaces the swear-words with a high-pitched bleep, imitating the noise sometimes used on the TV to bleep out*

swear-words. The actress can either make the
noise or simply say the word 'bleep'.)

SUSAN: *(As* ANGIE *again)* 'You haven't reckoned with me,
            you slimy *bleep*. I'm going to take you apart. I'm
            going to rip your *bleep*-ing head off. I'm going to
            bleep – bleep you in the *bleep-bleep-bleep*. You're
            going to be *bleep – bleep – bleep – bleep*, you *bleep
            – bleep – bleep (Long pause) bleep*.' *(She looks
            hopefully at* DIRECTOR*)* I think that works all
            right, don't you?

DIRECTOR: All right? All right? You missed out half the
            speech, and all because you won't swear! I mean,
            what is the matter with you? Everyone swears
            these days.

SUSAN: Just because everyone does it doesn't make it
            right.

DIRECTOR: What's wrong with it?

SUSAN: Well, it depends on the type of swearing.
            Sometimes it's just offends other people. Other
            times it offends God.

DIRECTOR: God? What's he got to do with it?

SUSAN: This word here, for example *(She points to the
            script)*. I don't believe in asking God to 'damn'
            people. I'll leave that decision up to him. The
            Bible says we should think carefully about how
            we use his name.

DIRECTOR: Look, it doesn't mean anything. They are just
            words.

SUSAN: If they don't mean anything, why are you using
            them?

DIRECTOR: Because that's the kind of language that Angie
            uses. I keep telling you. She's a rough diamond.
            From the wrong side of the –

SUSAN: *(Interrupting)* Tracks, I know. You keep on and on about railways for some reason. I can't see that makes much difference. I don't use that kind of language.

DIRECTOR: But it's not *you*, it's your *character*.

SUSAN: That doesn't matter. I've still got to say the words.

DIRECTOR: It's your *job*.

SUSAN: What difference does that make? My job is part of my life – I'm responsible for what I do during my job. Why should I have to do something I disagree with just because it's supposed to be my job?

DIRECTOR: Well, let's forget it then. You're obviously not right for this part.

SUSAN: OK. Well, I'm sure another part will come along soon.

DIRECTOR: Actually, I do have another play you might be interested in.

SUSAN: Really?

DIRECTOR: Yes. It's a children's play.

SUSAN: Oh, that sounds much better.

DIRECTOR: It's called *Little Miss Joyful*. You'll play the part of Little Miss Joyful – a colourful, happy character, who comes from the wrong side of the tracks.

SUSAN: *(Getting suspicious)* Sorry?

DIRECTOR: Armed with only her machine gun and her kickboxing skills, she goes around toytown ripping the heads off bad elves and brutally massacring naughty goblins.

(SUSAN just walks out.)

DIRECTOR: *(Calling after her)* You won't have to swear! Well, not much anyway . . .

TAKING IT FURTHER

Bible Background: Ephesians 5:1–4

1. Why do people swear? What purpose does it serve?
2. Are there different kinds of swearing? Is one more offensive than the other?
3. Do you think swearing matters? Or do you think it is 'just words'?
4. Do you think that Susan is right? Or is she making a lot of fuss about nothing?
5. Why should God mind about how we use his name?

32. We Haven't Got a Prayer

Topic: Prayer.

Characters: ONE – a soldier on sentry duty; TWO – another soldier.

Setting: A trench in a war. We don't know which war this is and, in a sense, it doesn't matter. It could be the Somme, or the beaches of Normandy or the desert outside Baghdad. It is morning after a night of shelling and gunfire. ONE has been on duty all night.

Props/costume: Two mugs of tea. A rifle of some sort. Army uniforms, if possible.

> *(ONE is on guard duty. TWO enters, bringing him a cup of tea.)*

ONE: Halt! Who goes there? Identify yourself! Put down any dangerous weapons immediately or I'll shoot.

TWO: It's me, and I've got two mugs of tea.

ONE: Oh, sorry.

TWO: Mind you, this tea is pretty horrible. I think you could reasonably call it dangerous. In fact, now I come to think about it, I don't know why we don't give up shooting at the enemy and set up a teashop instead. Although technically that would be a form of biological warfare. *(Handing tea to ONE)* Here.

ONE: Thanks.

TWO: So. You want to talk about it?

ONE: *(Puzzled)* Well, there's not much to say. It's brown and wet and occasionally hot. And I'd prefer it with sugar in it.

TWO: No, not the tea. All that just now. All that 'stand and deliver' business.

ONE: Oh. Bad night.

TWO: Yeah. It was pretty noisy.

ONE: I guess I'm a bit . . . a bit on edge.

TWO: You're not the only one. You know, I was lying awake last night, listening to the bombs and the explosions, and I was wondering, 'Is this going to be the night?' Is this the night I go to sleep and never wake up? *(He sips his tea)* Mind you, it wasn't all bad. At least all the gunfire drowned out Smithy's snoring.

ONE: I thought they were going to break through. I kept seeing things in the shadows. At one point I could see movement out there and I thought they were coming towards me. So I stood up and aimed and fired.

TWO: And what happened?

ONE: My gun jammed. So I'm left standing there, trying to fix it and praying, praying with all my might that I'd been imagining things. *(Pause)* Which I had.

TWO: You must be good at prayer then.

ONE: Never tried it before. I mean, it's not even as though I believe in all that stuff.

TWO: So who were you praying to?

ONE: Sorry?

TWO: Well, if you don't believe any of it, who were you praying to?

ONE: I don't know. Whoever it was, I promised him I'd change my ways, go to church, all that, if he'd just get me out of it.

TWO: It's funny, isn't it? I shouldn't think there are many blokes out here who haven't prayed at some time or other. Like they say, there are no atheists in the trenches. So why is it that when we're in trouble we all feel the urge to pray?

ONE: It's survival, isn't it? It's trying to get yourself out of a situation. And you'll try anything. I remember when I was young, sitting in school and praying as hard as I could that I would open my book and find that I had actually done my homework. That prayer wasn't answered, I can tell you.

TWO: Maybe. Some people pray all the time, though. Smithy, he prays. Reads his Bible. All that stuff. He prayed before all this.

ONE: Why?

TWO: It's what he believes. I guess if you believe God is real, if you believe God exists, then he might want to hear from you. I don't know.

ONE: Well, all I know is that it worked last night. I'm still here.

TWO: So. Are you going to keep your promise?

ONE: What?

TWO: Well, you said you'd made a promise. Swore to be good if he got you out of it.

ONE: Oh, that. I don't know. It was night. I was desperate. You know how it is. Promises look different at night. I'll tell you one thing, though.

TWO: What?

ONE: I'm going to clean my gun before I go on watch again.

TWO: Well, I'd better take over. And you'd better get some sleep.

ONE: OK.

(ONE *goes to exit.*)

TWO: Say a prayer for me, won't you?
ONE: *(Pause)* OK.

> *(ONE exits. TWO takes up guard and starts to watch the enemy. Freeze.)*

TAKING IT FURTHER

Bible Background: Philippians 4:6–7

1. Do you believe in prayer? If not, why not?
2. Why do people pray when they're in trouble?
3. 'I promised him I'd change my ways, go to church, all that, if he'd just get me out of it.' Do you think that the soldier should keep his promise? Do you think he meant it?
4. Do you think his prayer was actually answered? Have you ever seen prayer answered?
5. 'I guess if you believe God is real, then he might want to hear from you.' Do you think this is true?

33. Temper, Temper

Topic: Anger.

Characters: ONE; TWO (a woman); THREE; FOUR.

Setting: The characters line up across a bare stage. They address the audience directly, as if talking to a friend or acquaintance. ONE sits, as if driving a van or a taxi. TWO is talking on a mobile phone.

Props/costume: One chair. One mobile phone.

(ONE, TWO, THREE *and* FOUR *are on stage.*)

ONE: The thing is that, you know, you have to keep cool. It's no good getting over-excited and letting things get out of control. *(Shouts)* Oi! Why don't you learn to indicate, you stupid idiot! What do you think I am, psychic? Am I supposed to just sense when you're turning right? Stupid wally.

TWO: Well, I was talking to this shop assistant, and he said that they'd never received my order. Never received my order! I distinctly remember faxing it through last week. And I could feel my blood starting to boil.

THREE: I mean, everyone could see it was a foul. Our striker was pulled down in the box. I could see it, the crowd could see it, but strangely the referee didn't blow. So he's standing right in front of me and I let him have it. 'What's wrong with you, ref? Asthma? Not

153

enough breath to blow your whistle?' I mean, this is an important cup match. It could make or break our season.

FOUR: I don't mean to lose my temper. It's just all the demands. 'Be back by eleven', 'Don't go out looking like that.' It's like I'm living in a police state.

ONE: Anyway, what was I saying? Oh, yes. Keep your cool. That's the main thing. See, I'm a professional where driving is concerned. I'm a skilled technician. It's my job, after all. So you've got to put all things in perspective.

TWO: So I let him have the treatment. You know, the full-on shouting. I love doing that in a way, because it always makes people look so shocked. They think I'm this calm, quiet little woman and then I turn into a raging bull elephant. I really let them have it. People have always been surprised by my temper, because I look as though butter wouldn't melt in my mouth. My mother claims I was abducted by aliens.

THREE: So he turns round and says, 'I didn't think it was a foul.' Well, that was it. I mean no one talks to me like that. Red rag to a bull. So I says, 'Well, I thought it was a foul, you stupid, snivelling moron, and if you don't get with the action double-quick I'm going to stuff that whistle where you'll have a bit of a problem blowing it.'

FOUR: And what other weapon have I got? I've tried logic but there's something in the brains of parents that just doesn't work that way. They just can't see my side of the argument. So in the end the only thing I can do is scream and shout and slam doors.

ONE: Oh, what are you doing? *(Shouts)* Why don't you get on the pavement where you belong? Yes, I'm talking to you, you silly old man! Never mind 'zebra crossing'. Who's driving the van here, me or you? *(Suddenly calming down again)* It's for their own protection, really. You have to shout at them or else they might get hurt.

TWO: Anyway, I spent a good few minutes reducing this shop assistant to a quivering wreck, and then I spent a further five minutes screaming at the manager. You have to do a bit of shouting and ranting to get anywhere in this country.

THREE: And then he just walked off. Middle of the game. All the players still out there and he just said, 'I've had it with you,' and walked off. Walked off! I mean, what's the matter with the man? Doesn't he understand how important the local Primary School Championship is to our village?

FOUR: The other day they asked me to clear up my room. And I will clear up my room, but they want it right now. It's like everything has to be done in their time. *(Pause)* Anyway, I did clear up my room. I did it last summer. I remember because I found that swimsuit I was looking for.

ONE: Hot-tempered? Me? Nah. It's just the adrenaline, really. It's a jungle out there. Dog eat dog. You have to be first to that parking space or someone else will have it. It's a battleground. What else are you supposed to do?

TWO: And in the end they offered to give me a copy for free. *(Pause)* Sorry? What book was it? Oh, *The Little Book of Calm*. I mean, when you're faced with poor customer service, it's no good staying calm, is it? You never get anywhere like that. They just rip you off. What else could I do?

THREE: And the worst of it is that my boy looks at it as though it's my fault. He says that it was because I kept losing my temper. 'Well,' I said, 'I'm sorry. I'm sorry I feel passionately about winning. I'm sorry I'm a real supporter and not some half-hearted, lily-livered, prawn-sandwich-eating faint-heart like the rest of the parents.' *(Pause)* I've been banned from the touchline now. They say they won't let the children play if I'm there. They say I set a bad example, but it's how I'm made. I can't do anything else, can I?

FOUR: I don't mean to lose my temper, but it's just so frustrating! They are so unfair. What else can I do?

TAKING IT FURTHER

Bible Background: James 1:19–22

1. What kinds of thing make you lose your temper?
2. Are there times when losing your temper is a good thing to do?
3. If it's a bad thing to lose your temper, what else could you do?
4. Read the Bible Background. What kind of attitude is the writer urging us to take?

The Ernie and Frank Files

Ernie and Frank are two characters who have cropped up in a lot of my sketches over the years. Usually to be found in the pub, they refuse to let their innate stupidity deter them from discussing the deep, meaningful issues of life.

Frank is the more dominant partner. He is often opinionated, more certain and generally more worldly-wise (or at least as worldly-wise as you can be when you only have the IQ of a table lamp).

Ernie is quieter, more reflective, more questioning. It is Ernie's uncertainty that often undermines Frank's arguments. Not that Frank would ever admit that, of course.

Anyway, here are six of their appearances.

34. Come on, United!

Topic: Rivalry; hatred; tribalism.

Characters: FRANK; ERNIE.

Setting: A sports event. ERNIE and FRANK stand watching their team in action. They should follow the ball from one end of the pitch to the other. The imaginary sporting action takes place where the audience are sitting, so ERNIE and FRANK should face them.

Props/costume: Scarves, coloured shirts, hats. ERNIE and FRANK should be decked out from head to toe in red.

(ERNIE *and* FRANK *are standing on the terraces.*)

FRANK: Come on, you reds!

ERNIE: Yeah – come on, United!

FRANK: *(Sings)* You're not singing, you're not singing, you're not singing any more . . . *(To Ernie)* This is great – we're stuffing them!

ERNIE: Yeah . . . Nuffink better than stuffing the Rovers.

FRANK: That's right. *(Chants)* United! United! United! Come on, let's get another one! *(Sings)* We hate you Rovers, we do, we hate you Rovers, we do –

ERNIE: Er, Frank . . .

FRANK: Yeah?

ERNIE: Remind me again: why do we hate the Rovers?

FRANK: It's local rivalry, innit? There are only two teams in

159

this city, United and the Rovers. And we support United. So if you support United . . .

ERNIE: You have to hate Rovers.

FRANK: Exactly.

ERNIE: *(Pause)* But why?

FRANK: Look, don't keep asking stupid questions, Ernie. Just get on with shouting abuse. *(Turns to the pitch)* Oi, ref! Are you professionally stupid or are you just a gifted amateur?

ERNIE: It's just that, well, you know, I don't know about hating people.

FRANK: But they hate us.

ERNIE: Oh. I see.

FRANK: So we have to hate them.

ERNIE: Let me get this right: we hate them because they hate us.

FRANK: Right.

ERNIE: And why do they hate us?

FRANK: Because we hate them.

ERNIE: So we hate them because they hate us because we hate them because they hate us, because . . . *(Stops)* Ernie?

FRANK: Yes?

ERNIE: My head hurts.

FRANK: Look, it's a tradition thing. They hate us, we hate them. It's nothing personal. It's harmless. It's a tribal thing. It's something that binds us.

ERNIE: Wot, like eggs?

FRANK: Eggs don't bind us, Ernie.

ERNIE: They do me. I mean the other week I had the wife's Spanish omelette. I tell you, I couldn't go for days afterwards.

FRANK: That's not what I was on about. It's one of the things that marks you out as a true fan of United. You have to hate the Rovers.

ERNIE: Well, I don't like it. Why can't we be nice to them?

FRANK: *(Deeply shocked)* Nice to them? Nice to them?

ERNIE: They're just like us. They've all got mothers or children.

FRANK: Ernie, will you be quiet! They're not like us, are they? They can't be like us – it stands to reason – otherwise they'd be supporting our team. They are treacherous, shifty, lying and nasty specimens. I mean look around you, Ernie. Your Rovers supporter can't compare to the noble, intelligent, cultured supporters we have. *(He turns to the game)* Come on United, hack 'em down!

ERNIE: *(Looking at the game)* Oh, well played! Great pass . . . *(He stops, seeing FRANK's expression)*

FRANK: What colour was that player wearing, Ernie?

ERNIE: You've got to admit it was a good pass, though.

FRANK: What colour?

ERNIE: But –

FRANK: What colour?

ERNIE: Blue.

FRANK: And what colour strip do we wear?

ERNIE: Er . . . I'm not sure.

FRANK: Not sure?

ERNIE: I've got a sudden touch of colour blindness.

FRANK: You'll get a sudden touch of fist blindness in a minute if you don't stop this nonsense. For the last time, we support United; they support Rovers. We hate them; they hate us. Everything *we* do is right; everything *they* do is wrong. It's history, Ernie. It's been like that for centuries, and it will always be that way. If you want to stay one of us, you have to hate them. Anything else is a betrayal.

ERNIE: Well, if you put it like that.

FRANK: I do. Now, if you'll excuse me, I'm going to get a hot dog.

(*Exit* FRANK.)

ERNIE: I still think it's silly to get that worked up over a game of netball.

TAKING IT FURTHER

Bible Background: Matthew 5:43–48

1. Why does Frank hate the opposition supporters? What does he mean by a 'tribal' thing?
2. What do you think Rovers supporters think of United supporters?
3. Do you support a football team? Which teams do you like to see fail? Why?
4. 'Everything *we* do is right; everything *they* do is wrong.' In what other areas of life do you see this kind of thinking?
5. 'Love your enemies' (Matthew 5:44). Is this possible? What would the world be like if we did that?

35. Feet of Clay

Topic: Heroes.

Characters: ERNIE; FRANK.

Setting: A pub. ERNIE and FRANK sit at a table, sipping their drinks.

Props/costume: Table. Two chairs. Two pint glasses (part-filled, one with a cocktail umbrella in it).

> (ERNIE *and* FRANK *are sitting in a pub. Both have a pint in front of them.* ERNIE*'s has a little paper umbrella in it.*)

FRANK: I don't understand how he could do this to us.

ERNIE: No, Frank. I mean, we trusted him. We believed in him. I never thought he'd just . . . just leave.

FRANK: He has feet of clay.

ERNIE: Yes. *(Pause)* He can't go out much, then.

FRANK: What?

ERNIE: I mean, you couldn't go out in the rain, for example. Think of the mess on the carpet when you got back.

FRANK: What are you on about?

ERNIE: His feet. You know, the clay thing. You'd have thought with all that modern technology and all that they could have made them out of plastic or something.

FRANK: I don't believe this.

163

ERNIE: I suppose he had to wear wellies most of the time. You know, stop the water getting on them. And he couldn't have worn sandals in summer or else they'd have baked. He'd have had feet of pottery.

FRANK: Look, it's just an expression, right? I didn't mean he really had feet of clay. It just means that he wasn't the hero we all thought he was.

ERNIE: Oh. That's a relief. I thought it would be very inconvenient.

FRANK: That's the thing about heroes. They're never as heroic as you think they are.

ERNIE: You're not wrong there. You know, when I was young my hero was my dad. I used to look up to him. Well, I was only little, you see, but I also respected him as well. But you know, he wasn't the great hero I'd always thought he was. It was only years later that I found out he had a dark and horrible secret – something I never knew.

FRANK: What was it.

ERNIE: He was married to my mum.

FRANK: *(Sarcastic)* You astonish me.

ERNIE: Yeah, well, I was surprised. I mean, it's not exactly the action of a sane man, is it?

FRANK: So as I was saying, I can't believe what's happened.

ERNIE: You said that.

FRANK: I know, but what are we going to do? My whole world is shattered. He was going to lead us into the promised land. He was going to right wrongs. He was going to lead the fight against injustice. He was going to put everything right. And now he's deserted us.

ERNIE: You don't think you're taking this a bit too seriously? He was only a footballer, after all. He just got a good offer.

FRANK: Only a footballer? Only a footballer? He was Mr

Goalscorer. He was going to save the club. And now he's been transferred to . . . to . . . I can hardly bring myself to say it.

ERNIE: To the Rovers.

FRANK: To our hated rivals. Well, that's it. I'm not trusting anyone any more. I'm not going to go on believing in heroes. They're all the same.

ERNIE: They're only human, Frank. Maybe it's just wrong to worship them.

FRANK: They're all the same. They let you down.

(FRANK picks up the paper and starts to read.)

ERNIE: Well, perhaps you're right. Perhaps we should just stand on our own two feet.

(FRANK slowly puts down the paper. He has an expression of stunned surprise on his face.)

ERNIE: We look after number one. Heroes – you can't trust them. Isn't that right, Frank? Frank?

FRANK: Ernie. We've signed Ruud Van Owen.

ERNIE: No! I don't believe it! Ruud Van Owen! Ruud Van Owen! That's incredible! *(Pause)* Who is he?

FRANK: He's Mr Goalscorer. He's going to save the club. He's going to lead us into the promised land.

ERNIE: But you said –

FRANK: Ernie – that was totally different. Van Owen is a real hero.

(FRANK gets up and starts to leave.)

FRANK: *(Singing as he exits)* We love you, Ruudy, we do.

ERNIE: Here we go again.

TAKING IT FURTHER

Bible Background: Acts 14:8–20

1. Who are the people you admire? Is it right to have heroes?
2. What leads us to hero-worship?
3. 'They're only human.' Do you think that we expect too much of our heroes?
4. Read the Bible Background. What does the story tell us about hero worship?

36. Bending the Rules

Topic: Cheating.

Characters: ERNIE; FRANK.

Setting: A living-room. ERNIE and FRANK sit on a sofa watching the TV. It is probably better to stage this without a TV, but if you do use one, have its back facing the audience – that way you don't have to have anything on the screen.

Props/costume: Sofa. Nothing special as regards costume, although it would be fun to have ERNIE and FRANK decked out in their team's colours.

> (ERNIE *and* FRANK *are sitting on a sofa watching football on the TV.*)

FRANK: Come on, you reds!

ERNIE: Yeah – come on, United!

FRANK: Come on . . . down the line! Good lad, now take them on, run at them, he's doing it, he's into the box and . . . YEEEEESSSSSS!!!!

> (FRANK *leaps up from the sofa and starts punching the air in glee.*)

ERNIE: *(Pause)* He fell over.

FRANK: *(Stopping in mid-leap)* Fell over? Fell over? It's a penalty, Ernie! He got us a penalty! He took it into the box, ran past the defender and got the penalty!

ERNIE: *(Confused)* But the other bloke never touched him.

FRANK: Of course he touched him. He carved him down.

ERNIE: No he didn't! Look – they're showing the replay. The defender was three feet away. *(Pause)* Looking in the other direction. *(Pause)* Talking to his mate.

FRANK: Don't be stupid! He carved him down. He hacked his legs away. He . . . *(He trails to a halt as he studies the TV replay)* All right, maybe it was a bit of a harsh decision, but who cares, we got the penalty!

ERNIE: Yeah, but he cheated.

FRANK: Cheated? Cheated? That is Ronnie Rubin you're talking about. 'Rocket Ronnie' is a hero. He does not cheat.

ERNIE: *(Pause)* He fell over.

FRANK: That's not cheating. That's . . . er . . . gamesmanship.

ERNIE: Oh. I thought it was cheating.

FRANK: No, no, no, this is all part of the game. Everyone knows that players go looking for penalties. 'Rocket Ronnie' was just trying to get an advantage for his team.

ERNIE: Oh. So it's all right to lie and cheat, if it's going to get an advantage for your team.

FRANK: Yes. *(Thinks)* No. Look, it's not lying. Not exactly. It's a battlefield out there. You've got to take every advantage over your enemy. It's dog eat dog. If you don't eat them, they'll eat you.

ERNIE: It's a football pitch, Frank. It's not a battlefield.

FRANK: *(Mutters)* You haven't seen the way our defence plays. Look, it's just part of the game. It's accepted now. And when both sides break the rules, then the rules don't matter any more, do they? I mean, it's like there's the rules, you know, the ones that we're all *supposed* to obey, and then below them, there's the

real rules – the ones we *actually* obey. It's like speeding. You know: everyone knows that the rules say it's
illegal. But in reality everyone does it.

ERNIE: I don't.

FRANK: Yes, well, let's face it, your 1964 Morris Minor has
enough trouble getting out of your drive, let alone
speeding.

ERNIE: I still don't think it's right.

FRANK: But both sides do it! You don't imagine that if their
players went into our box they wouldn't try a dive?
Of course they would. They'd do a triple back-
somersault and end up in the stand. So we've got to
compete.

ERNIE: I see. So it's OK to cheat, because the other side is
cheating as well?

FRANK: Look, will you stop using that word! 'Bending the
rules' is not cheating.

ERNIE: What is it, then?

FRANK: It's . . . it's . . . it's creative thinking. It's strategy. It's
cunning. It's winning by every possible means.
Don't you understand? That player was only thinking of the team. Look at him now, still rolling on the
ground. Still in agony.

ERNIE: He's acting.

FRANK: *(Emotionally)* Yes, and he's doing it for you and me,
Frank. He's doing it for all of us. He's a hero to us
all.

ERNIE: Well, he's not my hero. I don't like ch– *(He stops
himself, as* FRANK *is glaring at him)* people who bend
the rules.

FRANK: *(Sarcastic)* Oh, don't you? Well, enlighten me, Mr
Purity, but what about our card game the other
night?

ERNIE: That was different.

FRANK: Oh, was it?

ERNIE: *(Defensively)* Yes. It was strategy. I was working to a complicated game plan. You know the stakes were high. I had to bluff.

FRANK: I asked you four times if you had Mr Bun the Baker. And you denied it every time. And at the end, what do we see? All the little Baker family nestling in your hand. Mr Bun, Mrs Bun and little Chelsea.

ERNIE: Yes, well, that's what I mean. I shouldn't have done it, Frank. That's what got me thinking about all this. I thought, if I can cheat my best friend, what kind of person am I becoming? I'm a bad man, Frank. A bad man.

FRANK: No, no, you're not. You're just ambitious. Committed to the cause. Win at all costs. Those are good qualities, Ernie. Those are the kinds of quality we need in our sportsmen. If they were all like that, then we'd . . . we'd win the world cup.

ERNIE: *(Reflectively)* And what does it benefit a man to win the world cup and to lose his soul? I read that somewhere. Or something like it, anyway.

FRANK: Success matters, Ernie. *(Starting to preach)* We've got to rediscover that spirit, that passion. We've got to be prepared to push the game to its limits and beyond. We've got to be prepared to exploit any weakness in the enemy, bend any rule to our advantage, do whatever it takes to –

ERNIE: *(Interrupting)* Frank.

FRANK: What is it?

ERNIE: He's just missed the penalty.

TAKING IT FURTHER

Bible Background: Mark 8:36

1. Have you ever 'bent the rules' in a game or competition?
2. Why do people act in this way? Are they forced to do it?
3. 'Bending the rules' is not cheating. Do you agree?
4. Frank talks about 'rules' and 'real rules'. Can you think of other examples where people don't obey the letter of the law?
5. 'Committed to the cause. Win at all costs. Those are good qualities.' Do you agree?
6. Jesus said, 'What good is it for a man to gain the whole world, yet forfeit his soul?' (Mark 8:36.) What did he mean by this, do you think?

37. Heaven Help Us

Topic: Heaven. Life after death.

Characters: ERNIE; FRANK.

Setting: A pub. ERNIE and FRANK sit at a table with their drinks.

Props/costume: Two pint glasses (part-filled). Two chairs. Table.

> (ERNIE *and* FRANK *are sitting in the pub with their drinks in front of them.*)

FRANK: Cheers.

> (ERNIE *sighs.*)

FRANK: Bottoms up.

> (ERNIE *sighs again.*)

FRANK: Down the hatch.

> (ERNIE *gives an enormous sigh.*)

FRANK: Are you all right?
ERNIE: It's Sarah.
FRANK: Sarah?

ERNIE: Yes. We've had some very bad news. It was too late to help her. She's . . . she's dead.

FRANK: Mate. I'm sorry to hear that. Were you very close?

ERNIE: We'd always been close. Right from the start, there was this kind of understanding between us. You know. A closeness. A kind of bond.

FRANK: I know. When did you find out?

ERNIE: This morning. It was hopeless. There was no cure. It was time to say goodbye.

FRANK: I don't know what to say. Had you known her long?

ERNIE: Ages. I was there when she spoke her first words: 'Who's a pretty girl, then?'

FRANK: Pardon?

ERNIE: I mean, I can't stand the grief! I'll never see her cheery face again. I'll never see her look in the mirror, or swing about on her little perch. I mean, yes, I had to clean out her cage every week, but she was worth it! I was prepared to make the sacrifice!

FRANK: *(Pause)* Now, correct me if I'm wrong, but would I be right in thinking that Sarah was, in fact, your budgie?

ERNIE: Well, yes.

FRANK: With whom you apparently had a very close relationship.

ERNIE: I'd reared her from a chick. I taught her to speak. She used to fly around the room and do her business on my head. Bonds like that aren't easy to break, I can tell you.

FRANK: No, I should imagine not.

ERNIE: I'm sorry. I . . . I'll pull myself together now. I must remember, she's gone to a better place.

FRANK: You mean the back garden?

ERNIE: What?

FRANK: Well, that's where you usually bury your pets, isn't

it? Just round behind the shed. You've buried tons of goldfish down there.

ERNIE: I was not talking about the garden. I was talking about the other place. You know, heaven.

FRANK: Heaven? What on earth makes you think that your budgie has gone to heaven?

ERNIE: Well, it stands to reason, doesn't it? There have to be budgies in heaven. There have to be budgies and doggies and all the good things in life.

FRANK: Don't be ridiculous. Heaven! There's no such place. When you die, you die. That's it. It's good night and straight off behind the shed to be buried.

ERNIE: I don't agree. I think there is a place we go. My auntie, she had a near-death experience, she did. She claimed to have seen a beautiful light which she was walking towards and she felt a wonderful warmth all over her body.

FRANK: Yes, as I recall it, your auntie's hot-water bottle leaked, causing her electric blanket to explode. I should imagine both of those had something to do with the lights and warmth.

ERNIE: You can mock, but I'm convinced. There is a heaven. Loads of people have had near-death experiences.

FRANK: Oh yes, and what's this heaven like?

ERNIE: I don't know . . . peaceful, I guess. Secure. Where you can be who you truly are and you don't have to worry about what's happening to you, or what people think of you. It's as if you took all the best bits of life and lived them all at one moment, all the time.

FRANK: And where do you get this from?

ERNIE: Well, I don't know. I always thought there was a place –

FRANK: Oh, yes. All that 'pie in the sky when you die' stuff.

You're *on* this earth and then you're *in* the earth and that's it. Heaven's just a sweetie to make us behave and be nice to each other.

ERNIE: No, it's more than that. I think it means that death isn't necessarily the end. It gives us hope. It means that we can all have a future.

FRANK: You're deluding yourself. You've been taken in by your auntie and her exploding electric blanket.

ERNIE: No. I don't believe you. I won't believe you. If what you say is true then everything is hopeless. We might as well just give up now. I believe that there is a heaven. I believe that, right now, Sarah is fluttering around, sharpening her little beak on some celestial cuttlefish.

FRANK: Face facts, Ernie. Sarah is gone. She has flown off into oblivion. *(Emphatically)* There is nothing after this life. Nothing at all.

(There is a pause)

ERNIE: *(Depressed)* Well, that's cheered me up no end.

FRANK: I'm sorry. But that's it. Only this life matters. There is nothing else.

ERNIE: Shame. I really hoped there would be a heaven.

FRANK: Well, it would be nice. I agree. But that sort of thing only happens in fairy tales.

ERNIE: Right.

FRANK: Cheer up! I'll tell you what – we'll go down the pet shop after this and I'll buy you another budgie.

ERNIE: *(Slowly)* No. No thanks. All of a sudden, I can't see the point.

(They slowly finish their drinks. Freeze. Exit.)

TAKING IT FURTHER

Bible Background: John 3:13–18

1. Do you believe in life after death? If you do, why?
2. What is your idea of heaven or hell?
3. Do you think a belief in heaven would make any difference to someone's life? How?
4. If there was a heaven, who do you think should be allowed in?
5. Read the Bible Background. What does this say about heaven?

38. I Want My DVD

Topic: DVD and CD piracy. Theft.

Characters: ERNIE; FRANK.

Setting: The pub. ERNIE and FRANK are sitting in their usual corner, drinking their beer. As usual.

Props/costume: Table. Two chairs. Two pint glasses (part-filled).

(ERNIE and FRANK are sitting at their table in the pub.)

FRANK: What are you doing tonight, then?

ERNIE: Oh, same as normal. Watch TV. Eat some crisps. Scratch myself. You know the kind of thing.

FRANK: Oh, right. So you don't want to come round my house to experience the latest, greatest, multi-media audio-visual sensation.

ERNIE: *(Pause)* Not again.

FRANK: What do you mean, 'Not again'?

ERNIE: Well, the last time you promised me an audio-visual extravaganza, it turned out to be looking at your holiday snaps of Paris while you waved some garlic around and your Brenda played the accordion. Not exactly hi-tech.

FRANK: Well, this time it is different. This time I have a Home Cinema system.

ERNIE: What's that, then?

FRANK: Picture this: 40-inch telly. Surround-sound speakers. And a brand new VDV player.

ERNIE: You mean DVD player.

FRANK: Oh yeah. I got one of those as well. I've got the lot. A complete Home Cinema. I've even got my Brenda selling popcorn in the hall. You interested?

ERNIE: I dunno. I never knew you were into all that stuff.

FRANK: What do you mean?

ERNIE: Well, your video collection, as I recall, consists of two Carry On films, some old episodes of *East-Enders* and the video of the 1983 Cup Final. Not exactly Barry Norman's 100 best films, is it?

FRANK: That's all changed now. I've got the latest VDDs.

ERNIE: DVDs.

FRANK: Them as well. I've got the new Star Wars/Dracula crossover.

ERNIE: *(Impressed)* Not *The Vampire Strikes Back*?

FRANK: The very same. I've got *Lord of the Rings Four – Hobbit with a Machine-gun*. And *Harry Potter and the Dungeon of Tacky Merchandise*.

ERNIE: *(Even more impressed)* Wow! But those films haven't even been released in the shops yet. How did you get them?

FRANK: I've got connections in the industry.

ERNIE: You mean you've been to that stall in the market.

FRANK: I don't know what you're talking about!

ERNIE: You've bought a load of fakes.

FRANK: *(Indignant)* They are not fakes! They are genuine imitations.

ERNIE: That's illegal.

FRANK: Legality, Ernie, is just a state of mind.

ERNIE: No it isn't. I mean, if I whacked you round the head with a frying pan, that would be illegal. And it wouldn't be a state of mind, would it? It would be a state of 'very big lump on the head'.

FRANK: No, but this is different, isn't it? It's not hurting people, is it? It's getting the goods cheaper.

ERNIE: But the people who made the real goods don't get paid, do they?

FRANK: Well, some people get paid.

ERNIE: Like who?

FRANK: Big Desmond who runs the stall, for one. And all the people in China who pirated these DTVs.

ERNIE: DV – Oh, forget it. That is not the point. These are illegal copies.

FRANK: Yes, and ask yourself, why do people buy them? It's because the legal ones are so flaming expensive. If they didn't rip you off in the first place, there wouldn't be a market. I mean, do you know how much it costs to make a CD? Pennies. And yet they churn them out at twelve, fifteen quid a time. No wonder all those kids swop those wossnames, those M3Ps.

ERNIE: MP3s.

FRANK: (Shouts) Whatever!

ERNIE: Well, two wrongs don't make a right. Apart from anything else, there's the quality. I mean, remember that Chanel Number 5 perfume you bought last year from that bloke outside the dog track? Smelt like Dettol.

FRANK: Yeah. (Pause) Actually it was Dettol. Brenda still wore it, though.

ERNIE: Yeah, well, no offence, but with your Brenda even Dettol is an improvement. But the point is, it wasn't the same quality.

FRANK: That's not a problem here. These are top-quality merchandise. Indistinguishable from the originals.

All right, there are moments when you can hear the director shout 'Cut!' and some scenes in the Harry Potter film that look like they were shot in a fog, but some would say that's an improvement.

ERNIE: Well, I don't think you should buy pirated merchandise. I think it's immoral.

FRANK: Suit yourself. So you won't be interested in the new James Bond movie?

ERNIE: *(Very impressed)* Not *The Spy Who Promoted Strategically Placed Brand Name Goods*?

FRANK: Absolutely.

ERNIE: *(Changing his mind)* Oh well, I suppose I could take a look.

FRANK: Come on. I'll tell Brenda to make some popcorn.

(They exit.)

TAKING IT FURTHER

Bible Background: Leviticus 19:11–13

1. Have you ever watched a pirate video or DVD?
2. Do you think it's wrong to buy these things? If so, why?
3. 'If they didn't rip you off in the first place, there wouldn't be a market.' Do you agree with this?
4. Do you think anyone is hurt by this practice?

39. Same as it Ever Was

Topic: Destiny. New Year.

Characters: ERNIE; FRANK.

Setting: What a surprise – it's the pub again! This time, it looks slightly more festive, or at least ERNIE and FRANK do. Someone has popped a party streamer over them and there are some of those paper party blowers on the table – you know, the kind that hoot and unwind and stop working almost immediately.

Props/costume: Paper streamers. Party blowers. Twiglets. Table. Two chairs. Two pint glasses (part-filled). ERNIE and FRANK each wear a paper hat.

> (ERNIE *and* FRANK *are sitting, as usual, in a pub.*)

FRANK: Happy New Year and all that! *(Raises glass)* Here's to the future!

> (ERNIE *does not respond.*)

FRANK: I said, to the future! To the New Year!

> (*Again,* ERNIE *does not respond.*)

FRANK: What's the matter? Aren't you drinking?
ERNIE: It's all too depressing.

FRANK: Sorry?

ERNIE: I mean, here we are, sitting in the same old bar, at our usual table. Drinking the same old drinks, doing exactly what we were doing this time last year.

FRANK: (*Cheerfully*) Not exactly the same. This year I am having new, barbecue-flavoured twiglets. I didn't have that last year.

ERNIE: That's it, is it? That's the sum total of how the world has improved this year? Barbecue-flavoured twiglets?

FRANK: What's got into you?

ERNIE: Well, you tell me, why should we be celebrating? I mean, not only are we stuck in the same jobs and living the same lives, but the world is as bad as ever. Last year, nothing but war and famine and death and disaster and gloom and despair. Nothing changes. The world is rotten to the core. Rotten, rotten, rotten, rotten . . . rotten.

FRANK: (*Pause*) You're a bit depressed, aren't you? Come on, Ernie-boy! What's the matter with you? It's New Year's Eve! This isn't like you! I mean, what about last year? You were dancing on the tables at this point. I remember, it was just before you got thrown out for using the darts board as a frisbee.

ERNIE: That was last year. I was younger then. I was naïve and innocent.

FRANK: (*Doubtfully*) Naïve and innocent? Are you sure?

ERNIE: I had hopes. I made resolutions.

FRANK: Sorry?

ERNIE: Resolutions. Last year I made some resolutions.

FRANK: Well, of course you did. New Year and all that.

ERNIE: I made resolutions. I . . . er . . . resoluted things. I resoluted that I would give up smoking.

FRANK: (*Pause*) Well, you cut down. A bit. On some days.

ERNIE: I resoluted that I would get more exercise.

FRANK: Ah, now, I have seen you doing that.

ERNIE: When?

FRANK: Well, you walk here every night for a start.

ERNIE: I only live next door.

FRANK: Yeah, but even so, you used to take the bus.

ERNIE: I resoluted that I would make this world a better place. And look at it! Has the state of the world changed? No. Still the same wars, dictators, terrorism, greed, meanness and disasters. And that's just at home.

FRANK: Well, I don't agree. You have made the world a better place.

ERNIE: I have?

FRANK: Yes, of course you have. Remember last week, when I was worried about that growth I'd found? You calmed me down. Helped me to realise that it was only a twiglet that I'd dropped down my vest the night before.

ERNIE: Well, I suppose . . .

FRANK: And then there was the time when you helped old Mrs Probate put her MFI furniture together. It's a wonderful coffee table.

ERNIE: It was supposed to be a wardrobe.

FRANK: But at least you tried, Ernie. At least you made the effort. You can't change everything at once. You have to do what you can. And maybe if we all did something then the world would be a better place.

ERNIE: Yeah. You're right, Frank. We mustn't give up. We can change the world.

FRANK: That's the spirit.

ERNIE: *(He drains his drink)* Now . . . Fancy a game of frisbee?

TAKING IT FURTHER

Bible Background: 1 Timothy 4:8–10

1. Do you make New Year resolutions? If so, why?
2. How do you feel when you look at the world around you? Is it getting any better?
3. What can we do to change things? Or are we powerless?
4. Do you have hope for the future? What do you hope for?

Some Bible Stories

The following sketches address the same kind of ethical and moral issues as the others in this book, but does so in the context of a Bible story. As soon as I started to write these 'Ready-to-Use Dramas' I decided that I would not retell Bible stories. I had spent years doing that already, and I had no intention of doing yet another sketch based on the Prodigal Son.

But the trouble about Bible stories is that . . . well, they're just very good. So, gradually, I found bits from the Bible creeping in. I found that characters and events raised exactly the kind of issues I wanted to address. I found, in fact, what so many other people have found across the centuries: that the Bible is about real life, here and now.

That is why all these sketches should be played in modern dress. Use suits, army combats, raincoats, jeans and T-shirts – whatever you feel makes the right impression. You don't have to dress all your characters in white nighties and tea-towel head-dresses. Audiences aren't stupid. They'll understand that what you're presenting is a modern translation.

The final three dramas in this collection are Christmas

sketches. I feel fairly confident in saying that I must have written more sketches about Christmas than anyone else in the history of mankind. Or at least it seems that way. Still, there is a constant demand and the story is so great, so marvellous, that there always seems more to say.

40. Brotherly Love

Topic: Sibling rivalry. Family relationships.

Characters: ESAU; JACOB.

Setting: The scene should be played with JACOB cooking. He sits by a camping stove, on which is a large pot. He is reading a book, breaking off occasionally to stir the pot. It's a kind of modern equivalent of the biblical nomadic life. Without the tent. And the sheep.

Props/costume: Cooking pot. Camping stove. Long-handled spoon for JACOB. Book. Bowl and spoon for ESAU.

(JACOB is sitting reading. ESAU enters.)

ESAU: Something smells good.
JACOB: *(Without looking up)* Yes. Unfortunately, it isn't you. Where have you been?
ESAU: Hunting, of course. Up in the hills. I killed two deer, three rabbits and a mouse.
JACOB: You shot a mouse?
ESAU: No. It was killed when one of the deer fell on it. Anyway, I'm starving! I need something to eat. I must eat! Give me food, do you hear? Food!
JACOB: *(Pause)* You're feeling peckish, then.
ESAU: Haven't you been listening? I'm starving.
JACOB: 'Starving' is when you are dying of hunger. 'Starving' is when the crops fail and the skies turn

189

black and you start to think about spit-roasting your grandmother. You, my dear brother, are merely hungry.

ESAU: What do you know? Do you know what it's like to spend hours up in those mountains? You get so cold you think you're going to pass out. I should know whether I'm starving or not. If I don't get any food in the next half-hour I . . . I'm going to die!

JACOB: *(Calmly)* Why do you have to make such a drama out of everything?

ESAU: I do not make a drama out of everything! *(Melodramatically)* I can't believe you just said that. That is the worst thing you have ever said.

JACOB: You're doing it again.

ESAU: That's because I'm starving to death, you idiot! Haven't you got anything to eat?

JACOB: Yes, thanks.

ESAU: Oh, great! What is it?

JACOB: Stew. Tender chunks of meat, stewed in red wine with vegetables and served in a rich gravy.

ESAU: Fantastic!

(He gets out a bowl and spoon.)

JACOB: What are you doing?

ESAU: Getting ready to eat.

JACOB: Why?

ESAU: You said –

JACOB: I said *I* had something to eat. I never said there was enough for *you*.

ESAU: Oh, come on . . . I mean, we're brothers.

JACOB: *(Pause)* And your point is?

ESAU: Well, we're supposed to love each other. You know, help one another out.

JACOB: *(Thinking it over)* 'Love one another.' No, no, I'm not with you.

ESAU: Oh, stop being so rotten! I've got to have something, or else . . . or else I'll die!

JACOB: Well, you know where the kitchen is.

ESAU: That's not fair. You know I can't cook. I don't do cooking. I kill things; other people cook them. That's the deal.

JACOB: Well, not this time. I suggest you head for the kitchen. You can probably find a cookery book in there. There's a copy of Delilah Smith's *Cooking for Hairy Hunters*. Look up 'sandwich'. *(Helpfully)* It begins with an 's'.

ESAU: You think you're so clever, don't you, Mr . . . *(He struggles to think of a witty insult, but fails)* – Mr Clever-clever-smarty-pants. *(Triumphantly)* Well, Dad likes me more than you.

JACOB: That is true. But then again, Dad has always been strangely impressed by your ability to kill small, defenceless mammals. Mum, on the other hand, recognises true quality. *(Smugly)* And, more importantly, she taught me to cook. *(Thoughtfully)* I'll tell you what. I'll do a deal with you. I will give you a bowl of stew in return for something.

ESAU: Not my crayons!

JACOB: No.

ESAU: My calendar of the 100 Sexiest Egyptian Women?

JACOB: No.

ESAU: Oh. Good. 'Cause I haven't got to Nefertiti yet.

JACOB: No, I want your birthright.

ESAU: What – the inheritance? The money?

JACOB: Money? You think I'm worried about that? No. I want the status. I want the rank of head of the family. I want to be the important one. Do you know what it's like to be with you and Dad? Always 'Esau this' and 'Esau that' and 'my son Esau the heroic killer of small mice'. Now it's my turn.

ESAU: You must be mad if you think I'm going to swap all that just for a bowl of stew.

JACOB: Suit yourself. I'm not the one who's starving. *(Sniffs the air)* Ahhh, smell that stew! I've put in extra herbs. *(Pause)* And I've baked some bread as well. *(Pause; ESAU is weakening)* And there is some pasta shaped like hieroglyphs.

ESAU: Ohhhh . . . All right, you can have the flipping birth-right! I mean, what does it matter? If I die I won't get anything anyway.

JACOB: I knew you'd see sense in the end. *(He offers his hand; ESAU pauses and then shakes)* A deal.

ESAU: A deal.

JACOB: Very wise.

(JACOB takes ESAU's bowl and fills it from the pot. ESAU starts to eat greedily.)

ESAU: *(In between mouthfuls)* Anyway, you got the worse part of the deal.

JACOB: I don't think so.

ESAU: I know so. You think that affection and status and all that can actually be handed over, like winnings in a game of cards. Don't you understand that all this will just make Dad hate you more?

JACOB: Maybe. But . . . but at least he'll have to take notice of me. At least he'll know I'm there. That's all I want. If people won't give, then I'll learn to take.

ESAU: Will we ever like each other?

JACOB: I doubt it. We're family.

TAKING IT FURTHER

Bible Background: Genesis 25:19–34

1. Do you have brothers or sisters? How do you get on with them?
2. What kinds of thing cause tensions in your relationship?
3. Would you talk over problems with your brother or sister? If not, why not?
4. Read the Bible Background. How would you describe the relationship between Jacob and Esau?
5. Many years later Jacob and Esau met up again. *(It's in Genesis 33.)* What has changed between them?

41. In the Public Interest

Topic: Loyalty. Peter's denial of Jesus.

Characters: ONE; TWO; THREE (they are all REPORTERS); VICTIM.

Setting: The stage is bare, but there is a constant movement from the three paparazzi-like REPORTERS, who constantly circle their VICTIM. You can inject some movement into this piece by having the VICTIM walk from side to side of the stage, trying to escape the REPORTERS. Of course, it is impossible to escape – they follow his every step. For obvious reasons, the VICTIM should be male.

Props/costume: Cameras. Flashlights. Microphones. Camcorders. The victim is dressed simply in working clothes – jeans and a jumper. He is not a rich or important figure. He is just caught up in events outside his control.

> (*The* REPORTERS *should surround their victim like vultures circling their prey. They are a mix of paparazzi and reporters, churning out a barrage of questions, armed with cameras, flashlights constantly going off.*)

ONE: (*Spotting the* VICTIM *entering*) There he is!
TWO: That's him!
THREE: Charge!

> (*They surround the* VICTIM.)

195

ONE: Have you heard the accusations?

TWO: How do you respond to the charges?

THREE: What have you got to say for yourself, eh?

VICTIM: *(Keeping calm)* I deny everything. I was nowhere near at the time.

ONE: So, you deny it, do you?

TWO: Trying to escape, eh?

THREE: How do you account for your movements?

VICTIM: *(Trying to joke)* I've always moved this way. It's an old boating accident.

ONE: Not that. People saw you in the city –

TWO: In the courtyard at the trial –

THREE: In the conservatory with the lead piping!

VICTIM: I wasn't there. I was at home.

THREE: *(Very loudly)* Ah-ha!

(Pause. They all look at THREE.*)*

THREE: *(Embarrassed)* Sorry.

ONE: We don't think you were at home.

TWO: We know you went out.

THREE: You were seen.

VICTIM: *(Flustered)* I went for a walk, that's all. I was looking at the stars.

ONE: It was cloudy last night.

TWO: Overcast.

THREE :   And very, very dark.

ONE: *(To* THREE*)* Of course it was dark – it was night-time, you idiot!

THREE: Oh. Er . . . a particularly dark kind of darkness. Probably an eclipse.

VICTIM: Why are you hounding me? Why can't you leave me alone?

ONE: Because we want to know the truth.

TWO: We have a right to know.

VICTIM: But what has it got to do with you, anyway? I mean, why does it matter what I thought or did? It's all over now.

ONE: The public demand to know.

TWO: Our editor wants the story.

THREE: These are major crimes.

ONE: State unrest.

TWO: Terrorism.

THREE: Double-parking.

TWO: We have a duty.

VICTIM: But I'm innocent! Look, other people got involved, not me. I mean, I have too much to lose – family, friends, career. I kept well out of it.

ONE: That's what you say, but you could be a cult leader.

TWO: A terrorist.

THREE: A Brownie.

VICTIM: Look, there is nothing different about me. I'm just the same as everyone else. I never had anything to do with it. But you – you make people think that I was involved and I'll be arrested! It's nothing to do with me. Just leave me out of it!

ONE: *(Moving in for the kill)* But we think you were with him.

VICTIM: No!

TWO: You smell of fish.

ONE: You speak funny.

THREE: You have strange movements of a boating-related nature.

VICTIM: *(Panicking)* I tell you, it wasn't me.

TWO: You were with him.

VICTIM: No!

ONE: You're a follower.

VICTIM: *(Desperate)* No, I'm not!

THREE: He trusted you.

VICTIM: *(Loudly and passionately)* I tell you, I never knew the man.

(There is a pause.)

ONE: *(Shrugs)* OK. If you say so. *(Looking at watch)* Hey – it's dawn.

TWO: *(Looking at watch)* Cock-crow.

THREE: *(Looking at watch)* Mickey Mouse's left arm is sticking up Donald Duck's nose.

ONE: The press will be rolling.

TWO: We've got to go.

(Exit ONE and TWO. THREE remains behind.)

THREE: Strange. I remember everyone cheering him. Now no one knows him at all.

(Exit THREE. The VICTIM is left alone on the stage. He buries his head in his hands. Freeze)

TAKING IT FURTHER

Bible Background: John 18:25–27

1. Read the Bible Background. Why did Peter deny Jesus?
2. Are there any times when you have denied your faith? Why do we sometimes 'play down' what we believe?
3. How do you think Jesus felt at the time? Read John 21:15–19 for Jesus's response to Peter.

42. Peace on Earth

Topic: Peace. Violence.

Characters: JOSHUA; ISAAC; JACOB.

Setting: A room. The sketch is set in Roman-occupied Palestine, around the time of Jesus. You could do this in one of three ways. You could have all the characters in 'traditional' costume, all flowing robes, sandals and tea-towels on their heads. Or you could have them dressed in army-surplus battle fatigues (combats). Or you could have them dressed in black suits and sunglasses as in *Reservoir Dogs*. The aim should be to convey the fact that these are paramilitary fighters planning a terrorist attack. Just not planning it very well . . .

Props/costume: Map or plan. See above for costume suggestions.

> *(The cast are huddled in a secret meeting. They have a map spread out in front of them.)*

JOSHUA: OK. So here's the plan. At six o'clock the Roman patrol will enter through the gate where Isaac here will be sitting, disguised as a leper. And judging by the look of him he won't need much make-up. He will then distract them, allowing –

ISAAC: *(Interrupting)* How am I going to distract them?

JOSHUA: Well, I don't know, do I? Create a diversion. Ask

them for money. Insult the Emperor. Engage them in illuminating conversation about Jewish customs. Just use your imagination.

ISAAC: *(Pause)* I don't know any interesting Jewish customs.

JACOB: I do. There's the one who goes down the off-licence and always pays for his wine with small mammals. The other day he tried to pay for two jugs of red wine with a rabbit and three hamsters.

JOSHUA: I said interesting customs. Not customers. Now, while Isaac is creating a diversion, Jacob will –

ISAAC: *(Interrupting)* Is he going to be there, then?

JACOB: Who?

ISAAC: This bloke with the hamsters.

JOSHUA: No, no, forget all that! There are no hamsters. There are only two Roman guards. And all you have to do is stop the Romans long enough for Jacob here to leap out and stab them with his sword.

JACOB: Problem: I haven't got a sword.

JOSHUA: What happened to the sword? You had it last week.

JACOB: *(Evasively)* I . . . er . . . I lost it.

JOSHUA: Typical. You'll have to pay it back out of your own money. In the meantime, use something else. Take a knife.

JACOB: That's no good. You try and get through Roman armour with a knife.

JOSHUA: Well, use another weapon. Use a club.

JACOB: A club? What do you think I am, some kind of barbarian?

ISAAC: How about a sling?

JACOB: No, I never could get the hang of that. I always had a problem with the release mechanism. Kept hitting myself in the eye.

ISAAC: *(Excitedly)* What about setting the hamsters on
          them?

JOSHUA: What?

ISAAC: Well, you know, that bloke with the hamsters, he
          could shout 'Attack!' and then all these hamsters
          would swarm over the guards and sort of . . . er . . .
          nibble them to death.

JOSHUA: *(Pause)* Let me get this right. You are proposing we
          kill two large Roman guards by employing killer
          hamsters.

ISAAC: It's an idea.

JOSHUA: It's a stupid idea.

JACOB: He's right. You couldn't kill a guard with a hamster.
          You'd need a ferret at least.

JOSHUA: Look, will you two shut up! You know what the
          task is. Now get on and do it. We have enemies to
          destroy.

ISAAC: *(Saluting)* Yes sir!

JACOB: *(Uncertainly)* Well . . .

JOSHUA: What's the matter now?

JACOB: Well, this isn't going to do that, is it? I mean, it isn't
          going to destroy our enemies.

JOSHUA: We're killing Roman soldiers.

JACOB: Yes, but then what? What happens when we kill two
          of theirs? They kill two of ours. Then we kill more
          of them and they kill more of us, and at the end of
          the day nothing changes. You've still got Romans
          on patrol.

JOSHUA: So what are you suggesting? That we should allow
          ourselves to be walked over? That we should allow
          our land to be taken from us? These people are
          tyrants. We have to fight back.

ISAAC: He's right. We can't just let them treat us like
          animals.

JACOB: No. But just because we're treated like animals doesn't mean we have to behave like beasts. Look, what if there was an even better way of destroying our enemies?

JOSHUA: Such as?

JACOB: Making them our friends.

JOSHUA: *(Pause)* You've been listening to *him* again, haven't you?

JACOB: *(Defensively)* No . . .

JOSHUA: Yes you have. You've been to hear him again. Every time you go it's the same. You come back with your head full of airy-fairy ideas. Last week it was 'Love your neighbour' – and you spent the whole week rushing up and down the street doing everyone's washing. What is this week's phrase, then? 'Be nice to Romans'? 'Lie down and let everyone walk all over you'?

JACOB: Love your enemies.

(Pause. JOSHUA is clearly stunned, ISAAC baffled. Then, enlightenment hits ISAAC.)

ISAAC: *(Excitedly)* Yes! I see now. You 'love' your enemies. You give them a big bunch of flowers. They smell the flowers. And then they die a long and painful death through hay fever.

JACOB: No! They don't die. Don't you see? As long as we all go on this way, nothing really changes. People keep killing each other and we all spiral downwards into oblivion. And throughout the ages nothing is going to change. Today we use knives, and clubs –

ISAAC: And hamsters.

JACOB: *(Ignoring him)* And tomorrow we'll use bigger knives and bigger clubs and . . . *(Runs out of words)*

ISAAC: Bigger hamsters.

JACOB: My point is the weapons may change, but the
           approach won't. We'll still be locked into the same
           way of doing things. Unless someone has the
           courage to put the weapons down, nothing ever
           changes.

JOSHUA: Well, if that's how you feel, you'd better go. There's
           no room in this organisation for people without the
           stomach for a fight.

JACOB: I'm sorry. I just don't want to do it any more.

           (He exits.)

JOSHUA: *(Shouting after him)* The fight goes on, do you
           hear? We'll kill the Romans, whatever your precious
           teacher says. And you still owe me for the sword!
           (To ISAAC*)* I can't believe it. He was our best, our
           fiercest fighter. Now what do we do?

ISAAC: Don't you worry, boss. I've got a secret weapon.

JOSHUA: *(Hopeful)* You have?

ISAAC: You see, we get this guinea pig and –

JOSHUA: *(Groaning, with his head in his hands)*
           Ohhhhhhhhhhh . . .

TAKING IT FURTHER

Bible Background: Matthew 5:9, 43–45

1. Why do people fight? What causes it?
2. 'These people are tyrants. We have to fight back.' Do you
   agree with this point of view?
3. 'We kill more of them and they kill more of us and at the
   end of the day nothing changes.' Can you think of areas
   of the world where this has happened?

4. How could people stop conflicts? What is necessary?
5. Are there areas of your life where you need to make an enemy into a friend? How could you do this?

43. Marching Orders

Topic: Telling the truth. Jesus's resurrection.

Characters: OFFICER; SERGEANT.

Setting: An army office. The OFFICER sits behind a desk, the SERGEANT stands to attention in front of him.

Props/costume: Chair. Desk. Beige office folder (sheet of typed paper inside). Envelope for the OFFICER. The actors are dressed in military fatigues (combats). If you can find an officer's cap, that would be great, but it's not vital.

> *(The OFFICER is sitting at a desk. The SERGEANT enters. He stands to attention.)*

SERGEANT: Sir!

OFFICER: What? Oh, yes, come in, Sergeant. Stand at ease and all that. Now then, I expect you know what it is I want to have a word with you about.

SERGEANT: I can explain everything, sir. The vat of wine had sprung a leak as I was transporting it to the officer's mess and I was merely trying to catch as much of it in my mouth so that it wouldn't stain the paving stones.

OFFICER: No, it's not that, Sergeant. It's your report filed here. On the disappearance. *(He picks up a beige folder.)* Now you write here, 'I was on duty with

Corporal Chalky when we started to feel all funny like.'

SERGEANT: Yes, sir.

OFFICER: That would be the wine, would it?

SERGEANT: No, sir. We hadn't been drinking. I never drink on duty, sir. Off duty, that's another matter.

OFFICER: I see. No drink then. Had you perhaps been taking anything else? Any other substance that would lead to hallucinations?

SERGEANT: Well, we had some of the cook's macaroni cheese in the mess before starting out. But I never heard of anyone seeing visions after eating the cook's food. Unless it were visions of having the cook stuffed with his own sage and onion.

OFFICER: So we can rule out food poisoning.

SERGEANT: I think so, sir. Speaking for myself, I was feeling fine.

OFFICER: I see. *(Pause)* Tell me, Sergeant, do you believe that there is life on other planets?

SERGEANT: I'm not quite with you, sir.

OFFICER: Aliens, Sergeant. Little green men.

SERGEANT: Do you mean Corporal Chalky, sir? Only he's not really green. It's just the mildew.

OFFICER: You don't think that you were witness to an alien abduction?

SERGEANT: Oh no, sir. I'd have noticed if they were green. No, the people we saw were white.

OFFICER: White.

SERGEANT: Yes. It's like . . . back in the old country, sir. The first snows of winter, high on the mountains. So white, it dazzles. Blinding. Like a white flame.

OFFICER: A white flame. Are you suggesting they were on fire?

SERGEANT: They weren't human, sir. Something burned

inside them. They was . . . holy. And strong! They picked up that rock like it was a feather.

OFFICER: I see.

SERGEANT: But that wasn't the frightening thing, sir. The frightening thing was the glow. From inside the cave. There was something happening there. Voices, sounds, lights . . . Well, we never stopped to look. We just fainted. It seemed the safest thing to do.

(The OFFICER *looks at the* SERGEANT. *He decides on a different approach.)*

OFFICER: Please sit down for a moment, Sergeant.

SERGEANT: Thank you, sir.

OFFICER: I'm sure you are aware that, were this story to get out, it could prove difficult for us. These are tense times.

SERGEANT: But it's the truth, sir.

OFFICER: Well, to quote the words of our esteemed leader, 'What is truth?' Truth depends on many unreliable things. Our ears and eyes can deceive us.

SERGEANT: I saw what I saw.

OFFICER: Yes, and what you saw, Sergeant, was a simple grave robbery. This man's supporters came and nicked the body, plain and simple.

SERGEANT: I see. So let me get this right, sir. There were no supernatural beings.

OFFICER: No.

SERGEANT: No lights, no . . . power.

OFFICER: Absolutely not.

SERGEANT: Just some women who overpowered two heavily armed guards and rolled away a three-ton stone.

OFFICER: *(Pause)* Listen, Sergeant. We all have choices in our lives. You can, of course, choose the honourable course. Or you can choose to serve your country. It's your choice. I am sure that, should you choose to stick with your story, it will provide you with a lot of comfort as you patrol in Caledonia.

SERGEANT: Caledonia?

OFFICER: It's in the north, Sergeant. The people up there are very hairy. Very savage.

SERGEANT: I see. And if I decide to serve my country, sir?

OFFICER: Ah well, then your country would be grateful. A nice posting near to home. A patrol job, maybe. Guarding the vineyards.

SERGEANT: I see. *(He thinks for a moment, but it doesn't take long)* In that case, sir, I think I ought to do the patriotic thing.

OFFICER: Good man.

SERGEANT: After all, my health hasn't been that good lately. I thought that the grave robbers were angels.

OFFICER: An easy mistake to make, Sergeant. You've been working too hard.

SERGEANT: Thank you, sir.

(The SERGEANT rises, stands to attention, salutes and turns for the door.)

OFFICER: Oh, one last thing before you go. Here.

(He gives the SERGEANT an envelope.)

OFFICER: It's just some back pay. To help you on the way home.

SERGEANT: Thank you, sir.

OFFICER: Oh, it's nothing. The usual fee – 30 pieces of
            silver.

            (The SERGEANT *salutes and leaves the room. The*
            OFFICER *closes the file and exits.)*

TAKING IT FURTHER

Bible Background: Matthew 28:1–15

1. Have you ever been 'economical with the truth'?
2. How would you answer the question, 'What is truth?'
3. Read the Bible Background. What are the implications
   for the Sergeant (and others) of telling a lie in this situation?

44. Pet Rescue

Topic: Obedience to God. Story of Noah.

Characters: ONE; TWO.

Setting: Outside a 'Pet Rescue Centre'. The stage should give the impression of a lot of DIY-style work going on: bits of wood, one of those folding workbenches, a tool box.

Props/costume: Saw. Wood. Workbench. Cupboard. ONE is dressed in overalls or a carpenter's apron. TWO wears a suit, carries a clipboard and is every inch the local official.

> (*Enter* ONE *and* TWO. ONE *is sawing at a piece of wood.* TWO *is officious-looking, with a clipboard.*)

TWO: Morning.

ONE: Morning.

TWO: Lovely day.

ONE: Can I help you?

TWO: Yes, my name is Smith. I'm from the Resident's Association.

ONE: (*Realising*) Ah.

TWO: You received my letter, then.

ONE: Yes.

TWO: Now, I'll come straight to the point. This Pet Rescue Centre you and your wife have been running. There have been complaints.

ONE: Complaints? What about?

211

TWO: We didn't mind when it was just the normal animals –
you know, rabbits and cats and dogs and all that. And
when you got in those badgers and the foxes, well, that
was a bit more extreme, but we were still OK. But now
it's getting out of hand.

ONE: What do you mean?

TWO: Well, let's take the hippos, shall we? Have you any idea
what smells the adult hippos can produce? No? Well,
maybe you should swap houses with the Bensons.
They live just over there. A few doors down-wind. And
I do mean 'down-*wind.*'

ONE: I can't help it – the hippos are an endangered species,
you know.

TWO: So are the Bensons. They can't sit out in the garden
any more without a large bottle of air freshener and a
pair of gas masks for emergencies. I mean, this is
Acacia Avenue, not the Serengeti. Cats, dogs, rabbits –
fine. You can even keep ferrets if you want to. But
hippos, no.

ONE: You're just being fussy.

TWO: And the same goes for the lions.

ONE: *(Outraged)* Lions!

TWO: At least the hippos only smell foul. At least the hippos
aren't carnivorous. One of your lions ate Mrs Jenkins'
poodle.

ONE: That was an accident.

TWO: *(Shouting)* It then ate Mrs Jenkins!

ONE: *(Irritated)* Well, she should have let go of the poodle.

TWO: Listen, 'Rolf', I don't know what you think you're up
to here, but it has to stop. The animals must go. And
another thing – the council are getting a bit concerned
about the size of your extension.

ONE: There's no need to get personal.

TWO: I mean, look at it! It's four storeys tall, for heaven's sake.

ONE: So what?

TWO: You only live in a bungalow! What do you want a four-storey extension for?

ONE: Well, you try getting a giraffe into a bungalow. He nearly broke his neck trying to bend down that far. I had to build something special.

TWO: It's ruining the neighbourhood. We used to have nice views of the countryside here. Now all we can see is a multi-storey animal house! It's got to go.

ONE: You don't understand. This isn't just a hobby. This is a calling. My wife and I have a mission from God.

TWO: God?

ONE: Yes. God told us to save the animals. God told me to build.

TWO: You're mad. It has to come down.

ONE: But the creator of the universe told me to do it.

TWO: I don't care if he is the creator of the universe. He still doesn't have planning permission.

ONE: *(Stubbornly)* It's not coming down.

TWO: Can't you see how unreasonable you're being? Can't you understand how unpopular this makes you?

ONE: I know all that. But sometimes you have to take unpopular decisions. Sometimes God tells you to live in a certain way.

TWO: Well, all I can say is that if you persist in this course of action, we shall have to take legal action.

ONE: Do what you must. I must do what I think is right.

TWO: Very well. I will see you in court.

ONE: I very much doubt it. Now, if you'll excuse me, I have work to do. Goodbye, Mr Smith.

TWO: Goodbye, Mr Noah.

(ONE resumes his sawing. Exit TWO. As he leaves, he holds his hand out, as if to test for rain.)

TAKING IT FURTHER

Bible Background: Genesis 6:9–22

1. Why is Mr Smith complaining?
2. Have you ever had to take an unpopular decision?
3. Have you ever felt under pressure to conform?
4. 'My wife and I have a mission from God.' How does your faith make you different?
5. How far should we go in trying to be 'popular'?
6. What kinds of thing might God tell you to do that would make you different from other people?

45. Tree's Company

Topic: Unconditional love.

Characters: FIREFIGHTER; ZACCHAEUS.

Setting: ZACCHAEUS is up a tree. The FIREFIGHTER is at the bottom. You can stage this by having ZACCHAEUS at the top of a step-ladder that has been suitably adorned with leaves and bits of real tree, or you could have ZACCHAEUS offstage and have the FIREFIGHTER simply shout up at him. Or, if you have one of those old-fashioned raised pulpits in your church, he could go in that. Or you could do it outside and have him in an actual tree (but be aware of health and safety issues here!). All that matters is that he is up the top and the FIREFIGHTER is down the bottom.

Props/costume: Axe. Tin (without a label of any sort). Other firefighting equipment, if possible.

> (*Enter* FIREFIGHTER. *He looks up into the tree and speaks to* ZACCHAEUS.)

FIREFIGHTER: What are you doing up there?
ZACCHAEUS: Er . . . Trying not to fall out, actually.
FIREFIGHTER: No, I mean, why did you go up there in the first place? Some kind of road protest, is it?
ZACCHAEUS: No, I came up here to get a better view.
FIREFIGHTER: A better view of what, exactly?
ZACCHAEUS: Of the procession. Of the teacher going by.

FIREFIGHTER: Couldn't you just have worn higher heels or something?

ZACCHAEUS: Look, I have enough people insulting me without wearing women's clothing. Now, are you going to do anything or not? I pay my taxes, you know!

FIREFIGHTER: And collect everybody else's, so I understand. *(Menacingly)* I didn't know you were a tax collector.

(FIREFIGHTER gets out an axe.)

FIREFIGHTER: Well, not to worry, sir, we'll have you down in a jiffy.

ZACCHAEUS: *(Panicking)* What are you doing?

FIREFIGHTER: I'm rescuing you. All I've got to do is cut through here and you'll be down before you can say 'Twenty-five per cent, please.'

ZACCHAEUS: You can't cut the tree down!

FIREFIGHTER: Why not?

ZACCHAEUS: I'm in it.

FIREFIGHTER: *(Pause)* And?

ZACCHAEUS: And what? Isn't that a good enough reason? You'll kill me!

FIREFIGHTER: Oh now, now, sir. I think you're overreacting a bit. I won't kill you. Injure, perhaps. Maim, quite possibly. But kill? I don't think so.

ZACCHAEUS: Look, I refuse to let you cut this tree down.

FIREFIGHTER: Well, if you insist.

ZACCHAEUS: Fine.

FIREFIGHTER: What about if I set fire to the base and then let it gradually collapse?

ZACCHAEUS: But I'd be burnt to death!

FIREFIGHTER: Is that a problem?

ZACCHAEUS: You are not to chop it down, and you are not to set fire to it!

FIREFIGHTER: Oh. Right. *(Pause)* I've got some dynamite in the van.

ZACCHAEUS: Look, just get a ladder! Just get a ladder and get me down. I've got to go and get a meal ready.

FIREFIGHTER: Meal, sir?

ZACCHAEUS: The teacher. He's coming to have a meal with me.

FIREFIGHTER: The teacher?

ZACCHAEUS: Yes.

FIREFIGHTER: The holy man?

ZACCHAEUS: That's the one. He's coming round for a meal.

FIREFIGHTER: Oh, dear, dear. I think we must have banged our head when we went up the tree, sir. Holy men don't consort with tax collectors.

ZACCHAEUS: What do you mean?

FIREFIGHTER: Well, let's just look at the facts – you are a slimeball tax collector whose job involves extorting money from the poor and collaborating with the occupying Roman army.

ZACCHAEUS: Er . . . Sort of.

FIREFIGHTER: He is a holy man, a teacher and healer who feeds the poor, gives sight to the blind, cures people who can't walk and generally zooms about doing good.

ZACCHAEUS: Yes.

FIREFIGHTER: Now, ask yourself, why would a man like that want to spend time with you?

ZACCHAEUS: I don't know. I mean, I was amazed when he saw me and told me to get a meal ready. I know I'm not respectable. I know that I've done some pretty bad things in my life. But maybe God loves me anyway. Maybe –

FIREFIGHTER: Hardly likely, though, is it? Hardly likely that God would have any time for scum like you.

ZACCHAEUS: All right, so I'm scum. So I've done some bad stuff. You think I don't know that? You hate me; everybody hates me. The trouble is, I hate me as well. But just for a moment today I looked down and saw someone who didn't want to spit on me, or beat me up, or shout abuse. Just for a moment I saw someone who really liked me and wanted to spend time with me. You don't know what that's like – when you think everyone is against you – to find someone who's on your side.

FIREFIGHTER: Well, I'm very glad for you, sir. Although I have to say, a holy man who can spend time with people like you is not so holy as he might be.

ZACCHAEUS: Perhaps he's a lot more holy than we think.

FIREFIGHTER: In the meantime, we have to get you down out of that tree. And I've got just the solution, although you might have to be a bit patient.

(He produces a tin out of his pocket.)

ZACCHAEUS: What have you got in there?

FIREFIGHTER: Woodworm.

TAKING IT FURTHER

Bible Background: Luke 19:1–10

1. Why did people hate Zacchaeus?
2. Have you ever felt that people were against you?
3. 'The trouble is, I hate me as well.' Why does he feel this way?

4. Read the Bible Background. Jesus got into trouble because of the people he was friendly with. Why?
5. Do you think God loves everybody? Is anybody excluded?

46. Fowl Temper

Topic: Anger. Righteous anger.

Characters: ONE; TWO.

Setting: The action takes place outside the temple, but there is no need to try to recreate that. (For a start, the area where the sellers operated had 162 marble pillars and a roof of cedar wood. And that's tricky to reproduce anywhere outside of Hollywood.) The easiest thing is to have the cast stumble onto the stage, as if they are escaping a riot.

Props/costume: None, really. ONE and TWO are market traders, so if you could get some of those market cash bags, that might help. Otherwise, they are the kind of traders you see touting their wares in any street market.

> (*Enter* ONE *and* TWO. ONE *is holding his head in his hands.*)

TWO: What happened?
ONE: What happened? What happened? I'll tell you what happened. I was struck on the head with a blunt instrument.
TWO: What kind of blunt instrument?
ONE: A chicken.
TWO: Sorry?
ONE: Well, I'm pretty upset about it, yes.
TWO: No, I mean, did you say 'chicken'?

ONE: Yes. A chicken. Brown. Lays eggs. Can be used –
       although this was a revelation to me – as a dangerous
       weapon.

TWO: It was a bit rough, wasn't it? I got a table on my foot.
       All my money went everywhere.

ONE: I mean, why do people get so angry? Why do they have
       to wreck the place? It's just senseless vandalism.

TWO: I agree. It's not as if we were harming anyone.

ONE: One minute you're sitting there at your stall, minding
       your own business. The next moment there's a riot
       going on and someone is chucking domestic fowl at
       you.

TWO: Anarchy. That's what it was. An anti-capitalist riot.

ONE: Exactly. Look at their leader. Gives great long lectures
       on peace and love. And then he comes in here and
       wrecks our market stalls.

TWO: I hope they throw the book at him.

ONE: I hope they throw the chicken at him. Give him a taste
       of his own medicine. You know what it is, of course.
       It's chariot rage.

TWO: You what?

ONE: Oh, yes. He was probably driving to the temple in his
       chariot and got cut up. Probably by one of those big
       white wagons driven by the couriers. And then he gets
       all steamed up, and all his statements about loving your
       neighbour go right out of the window and he storms
       into the temple and starts throwing chickens around.

TWO: *(Pause)* Why did you have chickens there anyway?

ONE: I'd run out of doves. You know – the sacrificial doves.
       It's a great little earner. People coming to the temple
       have to sacrifice something, don't they? And it has to
       be the right kind of something, doesn't it? So I sell
       them the right kind of sacrifice to please God. Only I
       ran out of doves. So I was selling some chickens.

TWO: Didn't people notice the difference?

ONE: Well, you can fake it a bit. Paint them white. That's how this happened. I was just down one end of my stall trying to teach this chicken to coo when that teacher bloke jumped on the other end of the counter, thus propelling the aforesaid fowl into my face at high velocity. What about you?

TWO: Oh, similar stuff. Money-changer. You know – people have to pay their temple taxes in the special currency. So I take their money and change it.

ONE: Good profits?

TWO: P-lease! It's not about profit. I am providing a public service. If people want God to forgive them they have to do it in the right currency. And if I happen to make a bit of money along the way . . .

ONE: Well, exactly. Nothing wrong with that.

TWO: No need to call us cheats and thieves. And as for defiling the temple itself!

ONE: Some holy man he turned out to be.

TWO: *(Pause)* You don't think he was right, do you?

ONE: Of course not. Look, he lost his temper. Everyone knows that if you lose your temper it's a sign you've lost the argument. There is never any justification for that type of anger and violence.

TWO: *(Convinced)* Yes, you're right. I shall make a full report to the temple authorities.

ONE: I'm sure they'll see our side of the story. After all, we didn't start the fight.

TWO: No.

ONE: Retain your dignity at all times. That's my motto.

TWO: Yes.

ONE: And never, never lose your temper.

TAKING IT FURTHER

Bible Background: Luke 19:45–48

1. What kinds of thing make you angry?
2. Is there a difference between 'losing your temper' and 'being angry'?
3. Is it ever right to take direct action such as destroying property?
4. Read the Bible Background. Why did Jesus act in this way?
5. What is 'righteous' anger? How do we know whether our anger is 'righteous' or not?

47. Dead Again

Topic: Life after death. Story of Lazarus.

Characters: LAZARUS; REGISTRAR.

Setting: A council office. The REGISTRAR sits behind a desk, writing in a ledger or large book. There are lots of files on the desk. LAZARUS enters and sits on a chair in front of the desk.

Props/costume: Phone. Files. Ledger. Desk. Two chairs. The REGISTRAR is dressed smartly. LAZARUS is dressed simply in jeans and a shirt.

> *(The REGISTRAR is sitting at a desk. There is a phone, files and a ledger on the desk. Enter LAZARUS.)*

LAZARUS: Er . . . Excuse me.

REGISTRAR: Yes, can I help you?

LAZARUS: I've come about a death certificate.

REGISTRAR: Well, you've come to the right place, sir. This is the Births and Deaths Registry. Sit down and we'll go through the details and issue a death certificate.

LAZARUS: No, no, it's a bit complicated. You see, I've got a death certificate already.

REGISTRAR: I see.

LAZARUS: But it's not correct.

REGISTRAR: Oh, well, don't worry, these mistakes will happen. You know, sometimes names get taken down wrong, or the dates need amending. I'm sure we can sort it out.

LAZARUS: No, no, all the details were right. Right name. Right time of death.

REGISTRAR: Oh. Well, was it a medical error then? You know, sometimes the doctors are in a bit of a hurry. We had a case last year where a young man was declared dead and turned out that he'd just been in a deep, almost catatonic, sleep. Mind you, they should have twigged – I mean he was an art student.

LAZARUS: No, no, the um . . . deceased person was really dead.

REGISTRAR: I don't quite see the problem, then. If he's dead and all the details are right –

LAZARUS: Well, things have changed, you see.

REGISTRAR: Well, perhaps you'd better sit down Mr, er . . .

LAZARUS: Lazarus.

REGISTRAR: Lazarus. *(Suddenly realising)* Hang on. That name rings a bell. I think I did a death certificate for someone like that a couple of weeks back.

LAZARUS: Yes. I'm feeling a lot better now, thanks. And I was just wondering whether I could have a refund.

REGISTRAR: You mean . . . You are . . . *(Shakes his head)*

LAZARUS: Yes. My sister paid the administration fee, as my next of kin, and Mary wants the money to buy some new perfume. She used the last lot up.

REGISTRAR: But this is impossible! I mean, I did all the paperwork. You were dead. You were definitely not in the 'art student' category.

LAZARUS: Yes. But as I'm not dead now, could I have my money back?

REGISTRAR: No, you can't! We don't have the mechanism for issuing refunds. We work on the principle that when someone has snuffed it, they stay snuffed. The bucket remains kicked. They don't come back from the dead.

LAZARUS: Well, I have.

REGISTRAR: How did it happen? No, don't tell me. It's that man, isn't it? The teacher? I knew it. That man is causing causing havoc with our filing systems. We've had people's servants suddenly leaping up and their daughters coming back to life. The Registrar of Blind People has got an office stuffed full of unwanted white sticks. And the Leprosy Registration Department can't keep up with all the changes. I mean, how does he do it? Who is he?

LAZARUS: How he does it, no one knows. He just can. Who he is – well, maybe you can draw your own conclusions. I mean, if you think it's all a trick, then he's just a con-man. If you believe that the dead really are raised, then he's someone else entirely.

REGISTRAR: Yes, well, I'm not paid to engage in theological speculation. The question is, what do you expect me to do about this certificate?

LAZARUS: Well, can't you just tear it up?

REGISTRAR: *(Deeply shocked)* Tear it up? Tear it up? I can't do that! I've entered it in the ledger now. It's on file. You can't just go around 'tearing things up'.

LAZARUS: But it's useless, isn't it? I'm not dead any more.

REGISTRAR: With respect, Mr Lazarus, that is your problem. As far as I'm concerned, the matter is closed. Death is certain. The only thing more certain than my department is the Department of Taxation just down the hall. People are born. They die. That's it. Nothing more.

LAZARUS: No, you're wrong. And I should know. I've been there. I've seen things that would make you hide in your own filing cabinet. Death is not the end. Oh, I know you'd like it to be all neatly parcelled up. Issue a certificate, put the official stamp on it. Game over. But that's not the way it works. And you'd better realise that before it's too late. *(Suddenly realising)* Hey – I've got an idea. If you can't rescind the death certificate, maybe you can give me a new birth certificate.

REGISTRAR: I beg your pardon?

LAZARUS: Well, that will work, don't you see? I was born. I died. Now I've been born again.

REGISTRAR: Oh, don't be ridiculous. Look, you get one birth, one death. You were born once and you can't be born again. You've died once – and you can't die again.

LAZARUS: No. You're right there. I don't think I can die again. Not really.

REGISTRAR: So, if you'll excuse me, I have work to do. And please tell your friend not to go around mucking up the system. Let this be an end to it.

LAZARUS: Well, I'll certainly tell him. But, as for 'the end of it', I don't know about that. After all, he hasn't died himself, yet.

*(*LAZARUS *exits. The* REGISTRAR *picks up the phone.)*

REGISTRAR: Hello? Miss Jones, would you mind getting me the file on Jesus of Nazareth. No, no, I just want

to keep it handy. I've got a horrible feeling it's all
going to get terribly complicated . . .

TAKING IT FURTHER

Bible Background: John 11:1–45

1. Do you believe in life after death?
2. Do you believe that anyone could come back from the
   dead?
3. 'If you believe that the dead really are raised, then he's
   someone else entirely.' Who do you think Jesus was?
4. 'I don't think I can die again. Not really.' What do you
   think Lazarus means by this in the sketch?

48. The Ante-natal Class

Topic: Virgin birth.

Characters: ONE; TWO.

Setting: The ante-natal class. ONE and TWO are two pregnant women attending the class. They lie on the stage and, throughout this sketch, engage in a series of exercises, as if obeying some unheard instructor. They are both heavily pregnant.

Props/costume: Two cushions for 'bumps'. Two floor mats. Two pillows. ONE and TWO wear loose-fitting maternity-style clothes or loose-fitting tracksuits.

(Two women are lying on their sides on the floor.)

ONE: So, when's it due, then?

TWO: The doctors say three weeks.

ONE: Doctors! What do they know? All they ever do is prod you about a bit and then give you some aspirin. When I first went to my doctor he told me I'd got wind. I said to him, I said, 'This is more like a hurricane, matey.' I knew what it was.

TWO: Well, that's what they say – three weeks. What about you?

ONE: Around the same, I guess. I mean, it can't go on for much longer. Look at the size of it! My old man said to me the other day, 'Delilah', he said, 'One day I'm

231

going to lead an expedition to rediscover the top of your stomach.'

(They change posture and start doing breathing exercises, both taking an extraordinarily deep breath and letting it out slowly.)

ONE: What a waste of time! Midwives! What do they know? All they ever do is rush round with towels and tell you to breathe. I mean, I'm hardly likely to stop breathing, am I? I'm hardly likely to get halfway through labour and say to myself, 'Delilah, time to see how long you can hold your breath for.'

(They take another extraordinarily deep breath and let it out slowly.)

TWO: Haven't you been doing your exercises, then? My Trevor says they're very important.

ONE: Oh, 'your Trevor' says that, does he? Men! What do they know? They stub their toe and it's a major medical emergency. My old man was off work the other day with a stomach-ache. I said to him, I said, 'You ought to try lugging around three bags of concrete in your lower abdomen. That'd give you something to complain about.'

TWO: Is your husband going to be present at the birth?

ONE: I'm not entirely sure he was there at the conception. I mean, he was there in body, you know, but his mind tends to wander these days. No, my girl, you don't want a load of men hanging about at the crucial moment. All they do is stand around looking guilty.

(They now sit up, occasionally lifting themselves up as if exercising their stomach muscles.)

ONE: Talking of guilty – look at her over there.

TWO: What about her?

ONE: Haven't you heard? Talk of the village. Only just got married.

TWO: Only just? But she's . . .

(ONE nods meaningfully.)

TWO: She's so young.

ONE : It's a big scandal round here. Still is.

TWO: Who's the father?

ONE: No one knows for sure. Oh, they tried to cover it up, but you know what villages are. These things get round. And anyway, after a while it's a bit obvious, isn't it?

TWO: Didn't the Rabbis investigate?

ONE: Rabbis! What do they know? Old, hairy blokes. Spend all their day poring over the scrolls and muttering about the Messiah. I said to them once, I said, 'Look, if the Messiah is coming, he won't come round here, will he? Not in this neighbourhood. Nothing but a load of workshops and stables. Hardly the place for the "Prince of Peace".'

TWO: Gosh – that was brave of you! They could have had you stoned.

ONE: I was stoned already – that's why I couldn't keep my mouth shut. I'd been drinking my old man's home-brew. That's got me into a lot of trouble, that stuff. Come to think of it, that's why I ended up here.

TWO: Don't you believe all that, then? All that about the Messiah? Don't you believe that one day the Son of God will come to earth?

ONE: Why would he come down here, eh? Don't talk to me about God! What does he know? What does he know about people like us? I mean, he's never been through this, has he? He's never been born, like us. He's never had to live, to sweat, to suffer pain.

(They finish their exercises and start to pack up to go.)

ONE: *(Looks across)* Look at her, smiling to herself. Like she knows some great secret and she's not telling.

TWO: Maybe she does. Maybe she knows why we put ourselves through all this.

ONE: Why? Because it's life, my girl. It's new life. Nothing can beat it. When you hold that little bundle in your arms . . . I don't know. All those teachers, all those wise men, what do they know? New life – that's the only thing that matters. That's the greatest present there is.

TWO: Yes. *(Pause)* I must go. Trevor's going to take me out to buy a new nappy disposal unit.

ONE: Why don't you use a goat like everyone else? They'll eat anything, goats.

TWO: No. Trevor wants to do things properly. It's very exciting, isn't it?

ONE: Yeah. Yeah, it's very exciting.

(TWO exits. ONE looks after her wistfully.)

ONE: New life. Oh, what do I know, eh? What do I know?

(She exits.)

TAKING IT FURTHER

Bible Background: Matthew 1:18–25

1. What kind of background did Mary come from?
2. What do you think other people in her town thought of her story?
3. 'Why would he come down here, eh?' Why would God come to earth?
4. 'He's never been born, like us. He's never had to live, to sweat, to suffer pain.' What if God had become a man? What difference would it make?

49. 'Tis the Season to Make Money

Topic: Consumerism. Christmas.

Character: MANAGER.

Setting: The bar of a hotel. The MANAGER stands behind the bar, cleaning the glasses with a towel. Bars aren't easy to create, because they are higher than normal tables. However, you can always place a plank on two high stools and cover the plank with a cloth to create the effect.

Props/costume: Counter. Glasses (one filled). Tea-towel. The MANAGER wears a blazer and a tie – a touch of the Basil Fawltys.

(The MANAGER *is standing behind the bar, cleaning glasses.)*

MANAGER: Look, I'm a businessman, right? I'm not in this for the good of my health. I'm doing it to make money. That's the name of the game.

I've got a hotel to run. I've got to fill the place. So if there's a time of demand, of course I'm going to cash in.

You don't understand – businesses like us, we rely on these occasions. After all, just for these few days a lot of people are going to be on the move and we've got to cash in. They're visiting friends and family, you see. It's a time when everyone goes home – well, they have to really,

237

don't they? You've got to spend this time with your families. It's expected.

So I don't need a load of holier-than-thou do-gooders telling me that all I'm doing is exploiting people. There are a lot of good reasons why the cost of my rooms have risen 500% this week. For a start, it's cold out – as you might have noticed. These rooms don't heat themselves, you know. I have to get people in to cut the logs, light the fires.

And it's winter, isn't it? No fruit hanging from the trees; no crops in the field. Food is more expensive this time of year. There's nothing I can do about that, either. We pride ourselves on the food here. Not like the Cat and Fiddle across the road. Appropriate name, if you ask me. They're always on the fiddle over there, and as for what they put in their meat pies – well, let me tell you, you won't get BSE from it. Fleas, maybe.

Not like this place. I run an exclusive establishment here. I mean we've got the lot. Hot baths. Fine food. Best Italian wine. Nothing cheap about me. I mean, take this bar. This is genuine veneer, this is. It takes a lot of money to fake something that well.

And another thing – there's a recession looming. It'll be here soon, you mark my words. The stock market is down, inflation is up, the currency needs devaluing and you can't get a plumber for love nor money.

So I have to take my chances. I didn't create this event. I merely get a bit of profit out of it. I know a lot of people are moaning about it and saying it's got out of all proportion. But I think this census is a good thing, and if it happens next year and the year after that and the year after that, so much the better. I can see it growing into quite a festival, you know. People travelling for miles to spend time with their families, bringing them presents, eating, drinking and all that. Lots of people in the bars, lots of people in the hotels, lots of people making pots of money. Good news for everyone.

It's like I said to that couple earlier: don't blame me for the census, I said. Everyone is full up; every inn is packed to the gills. You should have booked ahead. All it takes is a bit of common sense. I could see they didn't understand. Poor little thing. Looked exhausted, if you ask me.

Well, it was their own fault. Travelling all this way on a badly upholstered donkey, and her nine months gone. I said to them, don't blame me! Unless you can pay more than the rest of them there is no room. Even the Cat and Fiddle is full. Should make it smell even worse than usual. I sent them over there. I mean, if they're really desperate they can always sleep in his old cowshed. Probably cleaner than most of the rooms.

They said to me, 'Show a bit of goodwill!' And, you know, I almost fell for it. But I can't afford all that. This time of year isn't about charity. It's about making a profit. And if that means turning people away, well, that's life, isn't it?

Anyway, if you want bargain breaks don't come to me. This is a two-star establishment, you know. Not like them lot over the road. The only star they'll ever get is that one up there in the sky.

(Picking up a drink) Cheers!

TAKING IT FURTHER

Bible Background: Luke 2:1–7

1. 'We've got to cash in.' Do you think people 'cash in' at Christmas? If so, how?
2. Is it possible to challenge the commercialisation of Christmas?
3. 'This time of year isn't about charity. It's about making a profit.' Is it ever right to make a profit out of religious festivals?

50. Too Much to Ask

Topic: God's love for the outcast.

Bible story: Christmas: the shepherds.

Characters: ONE; TWO.

Setting: A hillside in the dark. If you can get hold of a brazier to represent a fire, that would be good. Otherwise, the shepherds are merely sitting, gazing at the stars and reflecting on the deep unfairness of it all.

Props/costume: The shepherds should be dressed as farmers – flat caps, wellie boots, a shepherd's crook or two (walking sticks would do). If you can get a stuffed toy sheep to represent 'Flossie', so much the better.

(ONE and TWO are shepherds, sitting on a hill.)

ONE: It's dark, isn't it?
TWO: Dark? You call this dark? You call this complete absence of light 'dark'?
ONE: *(Pause)* Yes.
TWO: This isn't dark. This is 'a bit dim'.
ONE: What do you mean? I can't see a thing. It's so dark that when I shut my eyes I can't even see my eyelids. Mind you, being as how the only thing I've got to look at is the sheep, perhaps that's a good thing.
TWO: You've got me to look at as well.

ONE: *(Pause)* Yes. Well, maybe the dark's not a bad thing after all. It's all right when you sit down here. It's when you have to go up into the mountains it's a pain. That's when you need the light. On the rocky terrain. In the hard places. *(Shivers)* Cold as well.

TWO: Cold? You call this cold? You call this very, very low temperature 'cold'?

ONE: *(Pause)* Yes. It's cold. Look at the sheep. Well, you can't, can you, because it's too dark, but if you could you would see that they are frozen stiff. Poor old Flossie there is frozen to the floor. She's leaning at a forty-five-degree angle with icicles hanging off her tail. *(Looks in his bag)* Oh. I haven't even got anything to eat. I'm starving hungry.

TWO: Hungry? You call this terrible, gnawing, empty feeling in the pit of your stomach 'hungry'?

ONE: What would you call it, then?

TWO: 'A bit peckish.'

ONE: Peckish? We haven't eaten properly for four days! The last hot meal I had was a very small potato three days ago.

TWO: I cooked last night.

ONE: Yes. Now, what was that again? Oh yes, I remember – rat.

TWO: *(Impressively)* Rat *flambé*.

ONE: It fell in the fire. It was not '*flambé*', it was just burnt.

TWO: I did a side salad.

ONE: Pond weed is not a side salad, no matter how much balsamic vinegar you put on it. It tasted foul. Oh, I'm fed up with this job. It's too hard.

TWO: Hard? You call this hard? You call this very difficult, underpaid, arduous, back-breaking work 'hard'?

ONE: *(Pause)* Yes. Of course I do.

TWO: This isn't hard. This is 'mildly difficult'.

ONE: *(Ignoring him)* I mean, you get hardly any sleep; you're always worried about wild animals, constantly having to go off and rescue the most stupid creatures God ever made – it's a terrible job. And what happens when you go down into town? People despise you. They treat you like dirt. Just because you're a shepherd. Oh yes, they're happy enough to eat your meat come Passover time. But as to talking to you, respecting you, just being nice to you, no way. We're outcasts. Just ragged, untidy, smelly shepherds.

TWO: Smelly? You call this enormously powerful body odour combined with more than a subtle scent of sheep-dip 'smelly'?

ONE: *Yes.* What do you think it is?

TWO: How about 'intriguing with a hint of menace'?

ONE: How about 'putrid and horrible'? What I'd give to be clean! To be washed. The only person who ever comes near me is the health inspector. And that's only to shout, 'Go away, you evil-smelling lump' through a megaphone. I could do with a hug.

(TWO moves towards ONE, arms outstretched.)

ONE: *(Hurriedly)* Not from you, you smell worse than I do.

TWO: Suit yourself.

ONE: It's not much to ask, is it? A bit of light, a bit of warmth, just to be clean, to have someone treat you like you mattered for once.

TWO: Not too much to ask? Not too much to ask to be clean and safe and cared for and made to feel important? Not too much to ask to be taken out of the darkness and into the light? Not too much to ask to be loved?

ONE: Yes.

TWO: *(Pause)* No. Not too much to ask. Not too much at all.

TAKING IT FURTHER

Bible Background: Luke 2:8–18

1. What kind of people are the shepherds in this sketch?
2. Why do you think people avoided them?
3. Why do you think God sent angels to tell the shepherds the good news?
4. 'People despise you. They treat you like dirt.' What kinds of people in our society today would feel the same as this? Do you think God has a message for them?

Subject Index

Numbers refer to Idea numbers, not pages.

Scripture Index

Numbers refer to Ideas, not page numbers.

50 Dramatised Bible Readings

by David Burt

Reading the Bible is one of the high points in any time of worship and teaching. Yet how much effort do we give to the delivery of God's word?

Experienced actor and scriptwriter David Burt gives a practical guide to the appropriate use of dramatic techniques in reading Scripture. Each of the 50 readings are given with full stage directions and tips for effective communication.

The full NIV text is provided, though the directions can easily be used in association with other translations of the Bible.

25 Sketches About Proverbs

by David Burt

A hen-pecked husband camps on his own roof for 16 years; Charles and Jennifer prepare for the end of the world; Adam and Eve hide apple cores from God; Ulysses the unicorn turns down a ride with Noah; the disciples argue over a tube of Pringles.

The book of Proverbs in the Bible has long been a source of wit and wisdom for people of various ages, races and cultures. So what better resource could we have for creating funny but poignant sketches about everyday life, using characters from biblical and modern times?

From subjects as diverse as betrayal, bullying, laziness and loneliness, there is something here for everyone!

Ideal for seeker-friendly services and all-age worship.

100 Instant Discussion Starters

by John Buckeridge

100 'strange but true' stories will get any group thinking, laughing, possibly outraged – but definitely talking!

- Fully indexed by themes and Bible references for ease of use.

- Questions and 'application' sections follow each anecdote, plus an extensive list of Bible references to lead into a group study.

- Includes guidance on how to run discussion groups.

- Excellent resource for cells or 'after Alpha' groups.

- Useful source of material for talks and sermons as well!

GREAT
IDEAS

50 Sketches About Jesus

by David Burt

Picture the scene: Jesus preaching at Wembley Stadium;
a paparazzi photographer in Bethlehem; Mary cooking
spaghetti hoops on toast; the wise men shopping in
Harrods.

Strange? Maybe. Funny? Certainly. But every sketch here
highlights a truth about Jesus of Nazareth that is relevant
to life today.

There's something here for all levels of expertise, and all
ages. Fully indexed by themes, occasions and Bible
references, this is an ideal resource for churches and other
groups who wish to communicate old truths in fresh
ways.

*'A bumper bran-tub of breezy curtain-raisers on a host of topics
which may particularly appeal to church drama groups with small
casts and limited resources.'*

Paul Burbridge, Riding Lights Theatre company

*'Dave is a natural communicator with a brilliant insight into
connecting with people right where they are. This book reflects his
unique skills and will raise many a theatrical curtain and no doubt
a few eyebrows as well!'*

Steve Flashman, Soapbox Communications